The Early Modern Englishwoman: A Facsimile Library of Essential Works

Series I

Printed Writings, 1500–1640: Part 3

Volume 5

Elizabeth Evelinge, II

Selected and Introduced by

Jos Blom and Frans Blom

General Editors

Betty S. Travitsky and Anne Lake Prescott

ASHGATE

Published by
Ashgate Publishing Limited
Gower House
Croft Road
Aldershot
Hants GU11 3HR
England

Ashgate Publishing Company
Suite 420
101 Cherry Street
Burlington, VT 05401–4405 USA

Ashgate website: http://www.ashgate.com

British Library Cataloguing-in-Publication Data
Evelinge, Elizabeth
Elizabeth Evelinge, II. – (The early modern Englishwoman : a facsimile library of essential works. Printed writings 1500–1640, series 1 ; pt. 3, vol. 5)
1.Poor Clares
I.Title II.Blom, Jos, 1948– III.Blom, Frans, 1945–
271.9'73

Library of Congress Cataloging-in-Publication Data
The early modern englishwoman: a facsimile library of essential works. Part 3. Printed Writings, 1500–1640 / general editors, Betty S. Travitsky and Anne Lake Prescott.

Library of Congress Control Number: 2002025881

The woodcut reproduced on the title page and on the case is from the title page of Margaret Roper's trans. of [Desiderius Erasmus] *A Devout Treatise upon the Pater Noster* (circa 1524).

ISBN 0 7546 0444 6

Printed in Great Britain by Antony Rowe Ltd, Chippenham, Wiltshire.

The Early Modern Englishwoman:
A Facsimile Library of Essential Works

Series I

Printed Writings, 1500–1640: Part 3

Volume 5

Elizabeth Evelinge, II

CONTENTS

PREFACE
BY THE GENERAL EDITORS

Until very recently, scholars of the early modern period have assumed that there were no Judith Shakespeares in early modern England. Much of the energy of the current generation of scholars has been devoted to constructing a history of early modern England that takes into account what women actually wrote, what women actually read, and what women actually did. In so doing the masculinist representation of early modern women, both in their own time and ours, is deconstructed. The study of early modern women has thus become one of the most important—indeed perhaps the most important—means for the rewriting of early modern history.

The Early Modern Englishwoman: A Facsimile Library of Essential Works is one of the developments of this energetic reappraisal of the period. As the names on our advisory board and our list of editors testify, it has been the beneficiary of scholarship in the field, and we hope it will also be an essential part of that scholarship's continuing momentum.

The Early Modern Englishwoman is designed to make available a comprehensive and focused collection of writings in English from 1500 to 1750, both by women and for and about them. The three series of *Printed Writings* (1500–1640, 1641–1700, and 1701–1750) provide a comprehensive if not entirely complete collection of the separately published writings by women. In reprinting these writings we intend to remedy one of the major obstacles to the advancement of feminist criticism of the early modern period, namely the limited availability of the very texts upon which the field is based. The volumes in the facsimile library reproduce carefully chosen copies of these texts, incorporating significant variants (usually in appendices). Each text is preceded by a short introduction providing an overview of the life and work of a writer along with a survey of important scholarship. These works, we strongly believe, deserve a large readership—of historians, literary critics, feminist critics, and non-specialist readers.

The Early Modern Englishwoman also includes separate facsimile series of *Essential Works for the Study of Early Modern Women* and of *Manuscript Writings*. These facsimile series are complemented by *The Early Modern Englishwoman 1500–1750: Contemporary Editions*. Also under our general editorship, this series will include both old-spelling and modernized editions of works by and about women and gender in early modern England.

New York City
2002

INTRODUCTORY NOTE

Elizabeth Evelinge

The title-page of *The declarations and ordinances*, an English translation of papal pronouncements upon the rules governing the convents of the Order of St Clare (see below), does not mention the name of the translator. However, her identity can be established on the basis of an entry in the dictionary of Franciscan authors compiled by the Irish Franciscan Luke Wadding (1588–1657). Fols Fff^{r}–Fff^{v} of the Appendix of Wadding's *Scriptores ordinis minorum* ['Franciscan authors'] mention 'Catharina à S. Magdalena' as the person responsible for three English translations. The originals she used were in all probability French texts, certainly in two of the three cases. The two translations from the French are *The history of … glorious S. Clare*, edited for the present series (2002) by Frans Korsten, and a life of St Catharine (forthcoming as Elizabeth Evelinge, III). The third one (the original of which may have been in Latin) is the text with which we are concerned at the moment.

'Catharina à S. Magdalena' was the name in religion of Elizabeth Evelinge, about whose life very few facts are extant. She was born in 1597. On 22 July, 1620, at the age of 23 she was professed as a nun of the Order of St Clare (also known as 'Poor Clares') at the convent of the order at Gravelines. In 1628 she moved to the new convent of English Poor Clares at Aire (see Korsten for a more detailed account of its foundation) and there she spent the rest of her life till her death on 23 September 1668. Her obituary in the 'Registers of the English Poor Clares at Gravelines' (Hunnybun, p. 52) has high praise for her exemplary life and for the care with which she carried out the various functions assigned to her; among these functions was the office of Abbess of the monastery, which she held for 25 years. Obviously, words of praise are a regular feature of obituaries, but in the case of Elizabeth Evelinge one of the qualities mentioned distinguishes her from all the other nuns: the fact that she had not only 'admirable guifts of her soul', but 'also a more polish'd way of writing above her sex'. The translation of *The declarations* at the age of 25 testifies to her skills.

The declarations and ordinances made upon the rule of our holy mother, S. Clare

As will be apparent from the body of the present introductory note, the history of the text that Evelinge translated is long and involved. Evelinge's original (to be found in Wadding's *Annales*; see below) is an attempt by two subsequent Franciscan General Ministers to formulate a detailed set of rules to be observed by the sisters of the Order of St Clare. Evelinge's 176-page English version was published by one of the most prolific presses of the 17th-century English Roman Catholic exiles, the English College Press at St Omer. The edition, which was presumably very limited, was meant for the English nuns living in monasteries in Flanders and Northern France.

The origins of the book that Evelinge translated go back to the year 1212 when Clara di Offreducio di Favarone (1194–1253), daughter from a noble Assisi family, ran away from home in order to become a follower of Francis of Assisi (1182–1226), the founder of the Franciscan Order. Inspired by Francis's ideals Clara opted for a monastic life of evangelical poverty and established a convent for women at San Damiano. Apart from causing dismay among her family, Clara's radical idealism created problems from the start with both the ecclesiastical and the civil authorities. The conventional choice for women who wanted to enter a convent was to join one of the established enclosed orders, such as the Benedictines. (The term 'enclosed' denotes that sisters and monks were not to have any contact with the outside world.) Although individual Benedictines took the vow of personal poverty, the monasteries themselves had possessions that provided the income with which to feed and clothe their members. The idea of a female mendicant order that, like its male counterpart, was completely dependent on alms did not appeal to city administrators who were afraid that they might be saddled with the responsibility of feeding the sisters when times were bad. The Church's reluctance to approve of Clara's initiative can be partly explained by the decision of the Fourth Lateran Council (1215) not to allow the foundation of any new orders. Other considerations that played a role were a fear of the excesses that the foundation of a non-enclosed female order might lead to and Clara's wish to place her order under the sole authority of the Franciscans.

What followed was a centuries-long debate about the various elements of the ideal way of life that Clara had envisaged for her own convent and the later ones to be founded on the San Damiano model. Apart from a whole series of papal pronouncements, this debate involved both pragmatic compromises and idealistic attempts to get back to the purity of Clara's ideals. Clara herself resisted a number of attempts to make her adopt a rule based on the monastic principles of St Benedict. In spite of opposition she managed to get papal approval of what she saw as the most crucial element of her ideal, the 'Privilege of Poverty'. In her view, communal poverty was not a self-imposed penance, but a gift, a privilege, that freed the community and its members from the bonds of materialism. This privilege was granted by Pope Innocent III in 1216 and confirmed by Pope Gregory IX in 1228. Clara, moreover, stubbornly went on to draft a rule of her own, based on the 'Form of Life' that had been given her by St Francis. Her determined efforts were successful when Pope Innocent IV on 9 August 1253, just two days before her death, gave his final approval by writing 'Ad instar fiat' ('So be it') on the copy of the rule submitted to him (*The Franciscan Experience*, s.v. 'The writings of S. Clare', 3.37).

Inevitably the rule as approved by Innocent IV entailed a number of concessions on the part of the sisters when compared to the spontaneous version of the youthful Clara, although part of these concessions can be explained as the result of making an individual ideal apply to a rapidly expanding movement involving the foundation of many new convents. Innocent IV's version of the 'Rule of St Clara' commanded strict enclosure, which contrasts with the picture sketched by Bishop Jacques de Vitry (c.1170–1240), who commented with admiration on the way of life of the 'Sorores Minores' ('Lesser Sisters' as a parallel to the 'Fratres Minores', the title adopted by the Franciscan brothers): 'They go into the cities and villages during the day, so that they convert others' (Armstrong, pp. 245–6). Furthermore Innocent confirmed that the responsibility with regard to the sisters was to be shared by the Franciscan Order and a Cardinal Protector appointed by the Pope. And finally, and perhaps most crucially in view of the later history of the Poor Clares, the Pope's approval of the Rule applied only to the convent at San Damiano: as opposed to the time-honoured rules governing Benedictine nunneries there was not to be a uniform 'Form of Life' that applied to all communities of Poor Clares, so that in the case of each new foundation individual decisions had to be taken about such matters as communal poverty.

Because Clara's 'Rule' in fact applied only to San Damiano and papal approval was required for later similar foundations, the subsequent history of the order is a very complicated one with individual houses or groups of convents adopting monastic regimes that sometimes differed quite radically from Clara's ideas. Examples are the rule allowing communal property given by Pope Alexander IV to Isabella of France, sister of Louis IX of France and foundress of the Monastery of Longchamps, in 1259, and the largely unsuccessful attempt by Pope Urban IV in 1263 to make all the sisters of the Order of St Clare adopt his own version of Clara's rule, a version that once again stipulated that convents were allowed to acquire property in common.

Almost one-and-a-half centuries after the death of Clara her uncompromising insistence on the 'Privilege of Poverty' found another advocate in the French Colette Boellet de Corbie (1381–1447). She chose to enter the religious life during a notoriously difficult period in the history of Europe and of the Roman Catholic Church, with two contending Popes, the controversies surrounding Jan Hus (1369–1431) and the wars between England and France in which Joan of Arc (1412–1431) played a historically prominent part. After successively joining the Beguines, the Benedictines and a convent of the Order of St Clare that followed the rule of Pope Urban IV, she set out to reform the Poor Clares by making them return to Clara's original principles. Her radical reformist ideas were backed up by the then General Minister of the Franciscans, Guglielmo da Casale (or 'William Cassall'), who led the order from 1430 till his death in 1442. He drafted a document that contained Colette's restatement of Clara's Rule together with a review of the various papal pronouncements on the matter. He submitted this document for approval to the Council of Basle and the papal delegates present at this Council in 1434. As soon as he had obtained the permission he triumphantly wrote to Colette informing her of his victory and he added a letter to all other Poor Clares present and to come recommending the adoption of this form of life (see the present edition pp. 4 and 7). The Latin text is substantially the original on the basis of which Elizabeth Evelinge – again nearly two centuries later – made the English translation that is to be found in the present volume. However, immediately before Evelinge went to work in 1622 the text underwent one more, minor revision.

This final revision was the work of another General Minister of the Franciscan Order, Benignus à Genua (1575–1651; see pp. 140–151 of the present edition). The changes that Benignus à Genua made to the text concern a slight re-adjustment of the division in chapters (Chapter I of his text forms part of the introductory letter in da Casale's version). Furthermore he numbered the clauses within chapters, made certain instructions more detailed (e.g. pp. 44–46), modified other instructions (e.g. the number of laybrothers a convent required, p. 57) and added traditional Franciscan devotional material (pp. 152–176).

Apart from these editorial alterations, there were a number of reasons why Benignus concerned himself once more with the Colettine rule. In the first place the cult of Colette (who was officially to be beatified in 1740 and canonized in 1807) was given papal sanction in the early years of the seventeenth century. In 1604 Pope Clement VIII gave the Poor Clares of Ghent permission to include the commemoration of Colette's date of death in the annual cycle of liturgical feasts, and subsequent Popes extended this permission to other convents in the next decades (Douillet, 397–8). Secondly, one of Benignus à Genua's primary concerns as General Minister of the Franciscan Order was to make sure that the Franciscan contribution to the history of the Roman Catholic Church was given the prominent place it deserved. It was for that reason that he asked Luke Wadding to start collecting material for an edition of Franciscan historical documents, which Wadding actually published in the years 1625 to 1654 under the title *Annales minorum* ['Annals of the Franciscan Order']. Thirdly, immediate problems with regard to the 'Privilege of Poverty' and the issue of the government of the Poor Clares once more came to a head, notably in the English Poor Clare convent at Gravelines (see Korsten). And finally, yet another reason must have been that in the early 1620s Benignus tried to reform the Franciscan order with papal support. This attempt met with fierce resistance in Spain and especially in France where an open revolt was backed by King Louis XIII and the Parliament of Paris.

One of the complications regarding *The declarations* not discussed so far is the fact that the first printed version of da Casale's Latin text dates to 1642 when it formed part of Volume 5 of Wadding's *Annales* (pp. 275ff). Thus we have a rare case of a printed English translation appearing 20 years before the first printed version of the original. Moreover, Wadding's *Scriptores* seems to suggest that Elizabeth Evelinge did not translate from the Latin but from the French. In the absence of a printed French version one can only speculate about the actual course of events. It is clear that manuscript copies of the rule must have circulated among convents from the days of Clara onwards: it is no use having a rule if it is not available to at least the abbesses whose duty it was to carry it out. Various catalogues and inventories of convents confirm this assumption. In the general catalogue of manuscripts in French libraries (see *Catalogue général*) there is a reference to an early 16th-century rule in French; Madan (Vol. II, Part I, p. 327, no. 2357B) contains a description of an English translation (for the use of the house of Poor Clares outside Aldgate) of a French equivalent in use in the Monastery in Paris (the text, a version of the rule established by Pope Urban IV, is printed in Seton). Other examples can be found among the manuscripts of The Huntington Library (Dutschke, pp. 328–329), in the works by Hoyoux (p. 152, no. 1065), De Kok (*passim*) and Goulven (pp. 266ff), and in the Bibliography of Lopez (pp. 460ff).

The absence of printed versions can be explained on the basis of the limited readership that might reasonably be expected: printers cannot have been keen to produce a book that would interest only abbesses of Poor Clare convents. The printing of an English translation must be seen as a move in a debate rather than as a commercially viable proposition.

If we turn to the work itself we get a fascinating insight into the daily lives of mediaeval and early modern Poor Clares. The 15 chapters comment on subjects ranging from abstinence, via the observance of enclosure and silence, to the election of abbesses and the care for the sick. A striking feature is the strong insistence on poverty, one of the original central issues of Colette and, as we have seen, one of the points of contention over the years. Very explicitly the rule states once again that no convent should possess land, vineyards, cattle or houses, nor receive rents or other regular income. The convents should have provisions only for short periods and no gold or jewelry. There are strict injunctions about clothing (only of the simplest coarse material), food (a completely vegetarian diet) and accommodation. In view of what was said above about the history of the order it can come as no surprise that much attention is paid to the issue of enclosure. Every care is taken to ensure that contacts with the outside world are absolutely minimal and the contacts that are necessary are regulated in great detail.

Also interesting are the rules concerning admittance of new nuns. One should be over 12 years old to be admitted to the convent, but only at the age of 18 could one be professed. The upper limit is 25 because after that it will be difficult to learn to read the Divine Office. This suggests that the convent was also a place where women were educated and learned to read. An exception is made for mature women who already possess enough education. *The declarations* further decribe the exact procedure when it comes to electing an abbess. It is a democratic process involving several rounds until one candidate gets more than 50 percent of the votes. Finally the austerity of the rule is balanced by a long chapter on the care for sisters who are ill.

There is only one edition of *The declarations and ordinances made upon the rule*, which one can assign on the basis of internal evidence to the English College Press at St Omer. Only one – very fragile – copy is recorded by *STC* and Allison (1989–1994) at the

Franciscan Library at Killiney. After the decision had been taken by the editors of 'The Early Modern Englishwoman' to use the 1975 'English Recusant Literature' facsimile edition of the Killiney copy of *The declarations* (see *Declarations* in the References) as the basis of the present edition, another copy was discovered in the Library of the Poor Clares at Galway. The latter copy is identical to the copy at Killiney.

The number of mistakes and printing errors is limited although the actual printing is not very good. There are spelling variations (such as 'byn' and 'bin' for 'been'), but variations of this kind and slight printing errors that cause no confusion have not been commented upon. On 44.4 'must as' should read 'much as;' on 64.2, 'an' should read 'any;' on 74.5, 'one consciences' should read 'own consciences;' on 122.1, '022' should read '122;' on 144.7, 'comfomable' should be 'conformable,' and on the same page, l.21, 'treatnings' should read 'threatenings.' On 145.16, 'drecting' should read 'directing,' and on 149.12, 'add' should read 'and.'

References

STC 5349.8

Allison, A.F. and D.M. Rogers (1989–1994), *The contemporary printed literature of the English Counter-Reformation*, 2 vols., Aldershot

Armstrong OFM, Regis J. (ed.) (1988), *Clare of Assisi. Early Documents*, New York

Catalogue général des Manuscrits des Bibliothèques Publiques de France, Tome XX, Arles (Paris, 1893), no. 63; see also Tome XXX, Lyon (Paris, 1900), no. 854 and Tome XL, Supplement (Paris, 1902), no. 985

The declarations and ordinances made upon the rule of our holy mother, S. Clare, D.M. Rogers (ed.) (1975), English Recusant Literature, Vol. 226, Ilkley/London

Dizionario Biografico degli Italiani (1966), VIII, 511–513, Rome

Douillet, Florimond-A. (1869), *Sainte Colette*, Paris

Dutschke, C.W. (1989), *Guide to medieval and renaissance manuscripts in the Huntington Library*, Vol. I, San Marino

The Fransciscan Experience, www.christusrex.org/www1/ofm/fra/ FRAmain

Goulven, Joseph (1952), *Rayonnement de Sainte Colette*, Paris

Hoyoux, J. (1970), *Inventaire des manuscrits de la bibliothèque de l'université de Liege*, Liège

Hunnybun, William Martin (ed.) (1914), 'Registers of the English Poor Clare Nuns at Gravelines', *Publications of the Catholic Record Society*, Vol. XIV, London

Kok, D. de (ed.) (1927), *Bijdragen tot de Geschiedenis der Nederlandse Klarissen en Tertiarissen vóór de Hervorming*, Utrecht

Korsten, Frans (2002), 'Introductory Note', *The history of the angelicall virgin glorious S. Clare*, The Early Modern Englishwoman, Series I, Part 3, Vol. 3, Aldershot

Lopez, Élisabeth (1994), *Culture et sainteté. Colette de Corbie*, Saint-Etienne

Madan, F. and H.H.E. Craster (eds) (1922), *A Summary Catalogue of Western Manuscripts in the Bodleian Library*, Vol. II, Part I, Oxford

Seton, Walter W. (ed.) (1914), *Two fifteenth-century Franciscan rules*, EETS, o.s., no. 148, London/Oxford

Wadding, Luke (1642), *Annales minorum*, Vol. 5, Lyon

— (1650), *Scriptores ordinis minorum*, Rome

JOS BLOM AND FRANS BLOM*

* We gratefully acknowledge the help of Father Ignatius Fennessey, OFM, librarian of the Franciscan Library at Killiney.

The declarations and ordinances made upon the rule of our holy mother, S. Clare (*STC* 5349.8) is reproduced by permission from the copy at Killiney. The text block measures 47 × 80 mm.

Readings where the copy is blotted or otherwise not clear:

63.19	approach
64.16	being
72.1	all
127.11	assigned
139.16	Basil
139.20	Heresies

THE DECLARATIONS AND ORDINANCES

made upon the Rule of our holy Mother

S. CLARE.

Permissu Superiorum. 1622.

HEERE BEGIN THE *Declarations, and Ordinances made vpon the Rule of the Poore Religious of* S. Clare. *First are ſet downe two Letters making mention of the Approbation, and Confirmation of the ſayd Declarations and Ordinances, written, and ſent by the Reuerend Father in our Lord, Brother* William Caſſall, *Generall Miniſter of the Order of the Friar-Minors. Of which Letters, the one was written only vnto his humble and poore Daughter* Siſter Collet, *the firſt Religious woman of the Reformation of the ſayd Order of* S. Clare: *The other in generall, both vnto her, & all the other Sisters of the sayd Religion. The tenour of the first is as followeth.*

VENERABLE, and deuout Daughter in God, health in our Lord Iesus, who is the true Spouse of virgins.] I haue receaued your letters & heard the relation of your Confessour, concerning the matter of the Confirmation and Approbation of the Statutes, which you haue sent, and caused to be presented vnto me: the which although they are very fit, and conuenient for the true obseruance of your holy Rule; neuertheles at the first sight of thẽ, they seemed to me to be in some sort difficile: wherfore as I was (concerning this matter) somwhat perplexed & troubled, I recōmended the affaire vnto our Lord Iesus Christ, and vnto the merits of holy Saint *Antony* of Padua, (vnto whome I would to God I were worthy to be deuout.) At length I was perswaded (as I doe verily belieue, through the merits of the sayd glorious S. *Antony*) that the aforesaid Statutes were especially sent from God. Wherefore I determined with my selfe, not only to confirme them, but moreouer also to Institute, Declare, & Authorize them. Thewhich we now send vnto you, & vnto your Daughters, instituted, declared, strengthned, & sealed with the Seale of the Order, togeather with the solemnities and assurances appertaining to such an affaire, both through the Authority of our Office and the Generall Chapter , as alſo through Papall and Apoſtolicall Authority which we vſe in this behalfe : exhorting and admoniſhing the ſaid deuout Daughters preſent & to come, that they receaue the ſaid Statutes with great deuotion , & humbly & effectually diſpoſe themſelues perfectly to keep them ; knowing for certaine that by the obſeruance of them (through the merits of the moſt glorious Father S. *Francis*, the founder of their holy Rule, and of the moſt worthy Virgin S. *Clare*, the firſt Plante of that moſt fruitfull field (to wit of the holy Religion) & moſt plentifully aboũding in vertues) they ſhall obtaine the plentifull reward of eternall life.

Visto

Vnto which Daughters, and first vnto you, I recommend my selfe; beseeching you and thē to vouchsafe to pray to God for me most vnworthy. Giuen at Geneua the yeare of our Lord 1434. the 28. day of September.

The Tenour of the second Letter, is as followeth.

BROTHER William Cassall, Generall of the Order of the Friar-Minors, and Maister in sacred Diuinity, vnto Sister *Colete* Religious in Iesus Christ, Foundresse of many Monasteries of the poore Dames of S. Clare Minorits, at this present time built & erected in the parts of France; & vnto the Abbesse, & all other Sisters of the said Monastery, and vnto all those other Cōuents present & to come, which vnder this forme and manner of life, shall be built & erected. Health in our Lord Iesus Christ the true Spouse of Virgins.] How much the great merits of the Noble virgin and glorious Lady S. Clare vnder Blessed S. Francis, Father & teacher of all Pouerty and holines, haue meruailously increased; and how those merits shine in the holy Church of God, and of the Spouse of Virgins our Lord Iesus Christ, doth not only appeare by the reward giuen vnto her in the Kingdome of Heauen, and by the holy degrees of the glorious Saints of Paradise, which do signify euerlasting rest; in which degrees, amongst the Prudent Virgins she is singulerly glorified & crowned: but

but alſo in this preſent time it is ioyfully declared, & made known by the great praiſe and worthy recommendation which is made of her in the ſaid Church of God, and eſpecially by the multitude of deuout virgins & other notable perſons, who in the order of her holy life and ſweet conuerſation, according to her example, in flying and leauing the perills of this miſerable world, do goe & run vnto the ſure and ſafe hauen of Religion: for the which we ought the more to giue thankes vnto God, by how much we ſee at this preſent, humane nature to be more enclined vnto euill; and that notwithſtanding through the diuine aſſiſtance, this holy Profeſſion doth not ceaſe alwaies to budde, & produce new plants, not estranged from the institution of the glorious Father S. Francis, & the traces and pathes of the glorious Mother S. Clare, who desiring with admirable feruour, that the Rule & forme of life to them giuen by the same S. Francis, and admirably obserued by their glorious Mother S. Clare, should be expounded and fortifyed with Declarations, and necessary Constitutions, that they may truly repute themselues imitatrices of so holy a Mother, & participate of her glorious merits; amongst whō, when I see & consider your Sister Collet before named, Religious, & Daughter in Iesus Christ (after the holy Lady) especiall Mother, & of these present writings, which are for the repose of their Consciences,

ciences, and safety of their soules, & also for the perpetuall strength of their regular obseruations, to be Patronesse & intercessour: We at your iust request moued & prouoked through your & their humble prayers, do by Apostolicall authority graunted to vs in this behalfe, send vnto you, both Abbesses & Sisters of Monasteries, by the grace of God & your meanes founded vnder the Rule & profession before named, & vnto all the Sisters of the other Monasteries, which in time to come shall be founded in the forme & manner aboue mentioned, these present Declarations, Statutes, & Ordinances to be perpetually kept: hauing maturely & with great deliberation bin made, & composed, & now authorized, as aboue said, by Apostolicall authority, & likewise by our Office, & the generall Chapter. Which declarations and Ordinances, are so much the more by you to be esteemed, feruently kept & obserued; by how much they haue bin more diligently viewed, examined, and notably approued by the most Reuerend Fathers in our Lord, the Lord Cardinalls of holy Crosse, & of Saint Angell, Apostolicall Legates, being actually present at the holy Councell of Basill, & by many other Doctours of diuinity; & also by many venerable Fathers, both for integrity of life & learning very famous: which Statutes & Ordinances doe heere follow.

First such Daughters & Sisters in Christ may doubt, whether by the

vow

vow they make at their Profession, when they promise to keep the
forme of life which is their Rule,
they be bound by commaūdment
to obserue the holy Ghospell, to
wit, as well the counsailes as the
commaundments: the cause which
may moue thē to doubt is, for that
in the said forme of life there is
three times mētion made, To keep
the holy Gospel: the first is cōtained
in the beginning of the forme of
life which saith; The forme of life
of the Order of Poore sisters which
S. Francis hath instituted, is this:
To obserue the holy Ghospell of
our Lord Iesus Christ, liuing in
Obedience, without Propriety, &
in Chastity. The second is, where
it saith: You haue espoused your
selues vnto the holy Ghost, choo-
sing

sing to liue according to the perfection of the holy Gnospell. The third is at the end, where it saith: Let vs perpetually obserue the holy Gospell which we haue firmely vowed. Vnto which doubt and cause thereof, we desiring to prouide for the consciences of the said Sisters, and take from them all difficulties which they may haue, in so much as is possible for vs to remoue and take from them; doe answvvere conformably vnto that which hath bin answered by many Popes, namely Pope Nicolas the third, and Pope Clement the fifth, vpon such like doubtes made by the Friar-Minors vpon the same points in their Rule; to wit, that the said Sisters by the vow which they make at their profession when they

they promise to keep the forme of life which is their Rule, are bound to obserue the holy Ghospell, in the same manner that our Lord hath deliuered it; to wit, all things which in the Gospell are commanded, they ought to keep as Commaundments; & the other thinges which are counsailed in the sayd Gospell, they ought to keep as Counsailes: & are bound also as vnto obligatory Commaundmēts vnto such Euangelicall counsailes which are put in their forme of life, vnder the word, or forme of commaundment, eyther negatiue or affirmatiue, or vnder words of as much force. But vnto other coūsailes of the holy Gospell they are not bound, but as other Christians are (excepting only, that in respect they haue willingly offered, and giuen themselues to follow the example of our Lord Iesus Christ, through the contempt of al worldly thinges, their Profession requireth, that they tend vnto greater perfection then other Christians.) Other thinges contayned in the forme of life, as well commaundments as counsailes, & whatsoeuer thing put in the same, through the Vow of their Profession, are not otherwise obligatory, then as in the same forme of life is specifyed; to wit, vnto Admonitions, as vnto Admonitions, vnto Informations as vnto Informations, vnto Exhortations as vnto Exhortations, & vnto all other things they are boūd in the same forme & manner as is there contained, & no otherwise.

Of

Of the Entry into this holy Religion.

CHAP. I.

ALTHOVGH that at the beginning of the second Chapter of the forme of life, it be contained, that the Abbesse may receaue any mayd for a Sister, with the consent of the greatest part of the Sisters, hauing had before the licence of the Lord Cardinall Protectour of the Order; neuertheles, we considering the former estate of this Order as being in the beginning founded very neere vnto the Court of Rome, & to the said Lord Cardinall, and being now so far of from the same; as also the strict pouerty of the said Sisters, & difficulty which they should haue to send vnto the said Lord Cardinall, to obtaine the said licence: considering also that the iurisdiction and gouernement of the said Order, hath bin fully, and wholy committed vnto the generall Minister and Prouincials of the Order of the Friar-Minors by Pope Innocent the fourth, and many other Popes: we therfore declare & say, that the said Generall Minister through the whole Order, and the Prouinciall-Ministers in their Prouinces, and their Vicars, haue authority to giue licence vnto the Abbesse to receaue for Sisters, such as flying the world are foũd to be fit, obseruing the manner which is contained in the forme of life.

1. We

1. We ordaine that according to the Ordinance of Pope Innocent the fourth, when any ſhall preſent herſelfe to vndertake this Religion (before ſhe change her ſecular habit and receaue the habit of Religion) there ſhall be declared vnto her, the moſt hard and difficult points which are to be obſerued in Religion, to the end that after her reception, ſhe haue no occaſion to excuſe her ſelfe of ignorance: and none ſhall be admitted, who for age, ſicknes, or fooliſh ſimplicity were not fully able to obſerue this manner of life;for by ſuch the ſtate and vigour of Religion, is oftentimes deſtroyed,or ſlackned.

2. Further,we will & ordaine, that the Siſters obſerue this manner in receauing any perſon vnto

the Order; to wit that when any is to be receaued, they first send her to some sufficient person out of the Order, fearing God, and louing the Poore, to the end by his counsaile her goods may be distributed vnto the Poore: and that the Abbesse and all the Sisters take heed, that neyther by themselues, nor by others they do receaue any of the goods of them who enter into Religion, vnles it were so small a matter, that those vvho should know of it, could haue no occasion to iudge sinisterly against them, or that she who entreth wold giue something vnto them, as vnto other poore, in manner of almes, to relieue their present, or neere-at-hand necessityes, and this comming from her owne freewill; for the

the forme of life doth require, that thoſe who enter be free, and doe with their goods, as God ſhall inſpire them.

3. The Abbeſſe and other Siſters ſhall alſo take heed, that for the reception of any perſon, they doe not permit others to doe by them, or by others for them, or for others, any couenant or paction, in which might be noted any ſpice of Simony: alſo they ſhall not permit that thoſe who enter do reſerue any of their goodes in the world, but that they offer themſelues wholy naked of all earthly thinges, into the hands of our crucifyed Lord: but if it ſhould happen that any one could not ſo ſpeedily diſcharge, & rid herſelfe of her temporall goods, and that ſhe

were no way content to returne againe vnto those thinges which she had so left; she shall in the best sort that she can possibly, commit the said goods in some certaine manner, vnto some persons fearing God, to distribute the same vnto the poore.

4. To the end, that in time to come the sisters proceed more Regularly; we ordaine that none be receaued vnto their forme of life, vnles they plainly perceaue, that she come vnto the Order principally for the loue of God, and health of her soule; and that she be not thereunto only moued by the sleight motions, or through persuasions, constraint, or feare of any person; but of her owne freewill, as being chiefely mooued there-

thereunto by the inspiration of the holy Ghost; and that they take great heed that none be receaued into the Order, except she be of a good will, and a faithfull Catholike; that she be not touched with any publike infamy; and that she be of vnderstanding, and of body sound; not suspected of any heresy; discharged and freed of her temporall goods; not bound with sentence of Excommunication or Interdict: but if it should happen that she were bound with the sayd sentence, that she be duely absolued before her reception, by the priuiledges heerupon graunted vnto the order of the Friar-Minors: neuertheles that they giue her to vnderstand, that if she returne againe to the world, she doth againe incurre the said sentence, and shall be bound therewith as before.

5. Item, that she be free, and not of seruile condition, to wit, a Prentise; or if she be, that licence of her Maister or Mistris be had; & that she be twelue yeares old before she be cloathed with the habit of Religion: and none shalbe receaued vnto the Profession before the 18. yeare of her age; for before that time she cannot be able to support & vndergoe the burthen of Religion.

6. We ordaine also, that none be receaued for the Quire after the 25. yeare of her age, except she were so cōpetently learned that she could learne to read the diuine office, without great labour or hindrance

vnto

vnto the others: also that none be receaued vnto Profession who cannot say by her selfe alone, or at least with others in common, the diuine Office: & that they receaue none vnto the Order, except it be manifest, that she haue liued honestly and well from the thirteenth yeare of her age, vntill the sayd tyme of her reception into the Cloister: & that none be receaued after the age of 40. yeares, except she were so Noble that her reception might notably edify the secular people, and Clergy; or that she were so ingenious and most strong that she were able to serue God, & the order according to your estate and forme of life.

7. Further that none professed of any other Order be receaued vnto

your forme of life without the licence of her Abbesse, or priuiledge from the Apostolicall sea.

8. In like manner we ordaine, that if the profession of any Nouice should be doubtfull before the end of the yeare the Abbesse in the presence of the Sisters shall make protestatiō vnto her, that although the sayd yeare should passe, she shall haue no right in the Religion, vntill such time as by mature deliberation they haue determined what they ought to doe, eyther concerning her Profession, or her returne to the world.

9. When they receaue any vnto Profession, she kneeling before the the Abbesse shall say leasurely with a high cleare voice in this manner.

In Nomine Patris; & Filij: & Spiritus Sancti. Amen.

I Sister N. doe Vow vnto Almighty God; vnto the glorious virgin Mary; vnto our holy Father S. Francis; *vnto our holy Mother S.* Clare; *and vnto all the holy Saints; and vnto you Reuerend*

Mother

Mother Abbeſſe, *and vnto all your ſucceſſours ſucceeding in your place; to obſerue all the tyme of my life, the Rule and forme of life of the Poore Siſters of S.* Clare, *which hath bin giuen by S.* Francis *vnto the ſayd Saint* Clare,*and hath bin Confirmed by our holy Father Pope* Innocent *the Fourth, liuing in*

O B E-

OBEDIENCE, without PROPRIETY, *and in* CHASTITY, *alſo obſeruing* CLOISTER, *according to the Ordinance of the ſayd Rule.*

Then the Abbeſſe who doth receaue her, doth promiſe vnto her (if ſhe do obſerue that which ſhe hath vowed) the eternall life.

10. We alſo ordayne, that at the Cloathing, the hayre be cut off round, and aboue the eares, & that after that tyme they doe neuer ſu-

ffer their hayre to grow long: but that often in the yeare, by the appointment of the Abbesse, all the Sisters alike haue their hayre cut; except that for some sicknes or weaknes it were thought conuenient to do otherwise.

Of the quality of their Habits, and of their Garments.

CHAP. II.

VVHEREAS it is contained in the Rule, and forme of life, that the Sisters be cloathed with poore and vile cloathes.

1. We ordayne, and determine, that this vility be vnderstood concer-

concerning the price & the colour, and although that it be contayned in the sayd forme of life of those who enter into this Religion, that the secular Habit being taken away the Abbesse shall lend her three coates and one cloake; neuertheles if necessity, or sicknes, or the conditiō of the person, or of the place, or of the tyme, should cause any of them to haue neede of more coates; we declare that the Abbesse (vvith counsayle of the Discreet) may duely prouide for those who haue the said necessity, considering that the sayd forme of life doth also say, that the Abbesse shall discreetly prouide her Sisters of cloathes, according vnto the quality of the persons, of the places, of the tymes, and of the cold regions, like

like as she shall see it to be expedient vnto their necessityes.

2. It is to be vnderstood that the three coates which are expressed in the forme of life, ought not to be all of one forme and fashion; for the two vnder-coates are graunted them, only for warmth and for the decency of the body, nor is there obligation or need they be al of one colour.

3. Therfore we will and ordayne, that the vppermost coate be called the habit of the Order, without which it is not lawfull for any of the sisters to goe, or to be seene in publike, or to sleep, vnles for sicknes, weaknes, or other manifest necessity it be othervvise iudged expedient by the Abbesse or Vicaresse, with the cõsent of the greatest

part

part of the discreet.

4. The habit shall not be so lōg that it traine on the ground vpon the Sister that weareth it; and in largenes it shall not passe the measure of 14. palmes; the length of the sleeues, shal be but to the knockles of the hands.

5. The vnder coates shall be of vile and course cloath, and shall not be doubled with furres. The cloake also shal be of vile & course cloath, and shall not be curiously gathered or pleighted about the necke, nor so long that it traine on the ground: but alwaies in all their garments shall manifestly appeare austerity, vility, and Pouerty, both in the manner of making, price, and colour; and in this sort both the Abbesse, and the sisters

in office, and all the other Sisters, shall be cloathed vvith common cloath without any partiality. The corde with which the sisters girde themselues shall be common, vile, without any curiosity.

6. Furthermore we appoint and ordaine, that all the sisters as well the Abbesse as the other sisters without any difference, couer their heades in all humility, decency, & Religiosity, without any curiosity, or vanity: and to the end that this be the better kept and obserued of the sisters, & of all their Couents, we ordayne that all the Sisters shall in such sort put on their kerchers, that their fore-head, cheekes, and chinne may be for the most part couered, in such sort that none may euer see them in the full face; as al-

so their kerchers, and their veyles shall be so large, and put on in such sort that their whole head, & their breast, & shoulders be for the most part couered.

7. Also, we will that all their veiles and kerchers be of course cloath, to the end that in them doe alwayes appeare the holy pouerty and austerity of their Profession.

8. Furthermore, we doe allow that euery Sister (vvith the consent of the Abbesse) may haue two blacke veyles, and white kerchers, to chaunge them, and keep themselues alwayes cleane, & decent. And that the Sisters take great heed that they neuer haue any kercher pleighted or curiously folded, nor their veiles of silke, nor any other costly stuffe.

9. No Nouice ſhall weare the blacke veile, before ſhe haue expreſly made her profeſſion, except ſhe were before profeſſed in another Religion; but ſhall weare the white kercher decently put on, according to the appointment of the Abbeſſe, & as it hath byn alwayes vnto this time accuſtomed.

10. To the end our beddes be like vnto that, on which he dyed, who ſayth, The foxes haue their holes, and the birdes of the ayre their neſtes, but the Sonne of man hath not vvhereupon to reſt his head; and to be alſo more wakefull and diligent to riſe vnto Mattins, and to be conformable vnto our holy Mother S. Clare, who oftentimes lay on the bare ground, or rather vnto Ieſus Chriſt the holy

of

of Holies, who had no other bed then the sharp desert; we ordaine that no sister (if she be not sicke or very weak) do sleep otherwise then only vpon a sack filled with straw, with cōuenient couerlets according to the discretion of the Abbesse: but vvith the sicke the Abbesse ought charitably to dispence, as it is contained in the Rule and forme of life.

11. Further we ordayne, that according to the example of Iesus Christ, and the glorious virgin S. Clare, the sisters goe bare-foote in signe of Humility, Pouerty, and mortification of the sensuality, contenting themselues only with wodden pattens vnder their feete, hauing a list nailed aboue to hold thē on.

Of the diuine Office.

CHAP. III.

CONCERNING the diuine Office which they must pay vnto God as well by day as by night, let this be obserued; that before all the Canonicall houres, immediatly after the first peale is ronge, all the sisters shall come into the quire to prepare their harts for our Lord, except they were lawfully excused in some affaire which could not be deferred, and that according to the iudgment of the Abbesse or her Vicaresse, and there they shall remaine without going or comming, or without laughing, making

making noise, or vainly looking a-bout, but perseuere all togeather vvith one courage in peace, silence, Religious grauity, and due reuerence.

2. That none presume to goe forth of the Quire so long as the diuine Office is a reading, except they haue licence of the Abbesse, or her Vicaresse, or of her who presents her place, vntill the whole Office be accomplished.

3. We exhort all the Sisters in our Lord Iesus Christ, that alwayes & in all places they accomplish the diuine office attentiuely, distinctly, entierly, and Religiously; and they must begin and make their stops togeather; they must also with one and the like courage perseuere vnto the end, in such sort that the

great Office be alwaies said higher and more leasurely then the office of our Blessed Lady, and that of the Dead.

4. Concerning the mãner to ring vnto Masse, as vnto the Canonicall houres, and the manner of siting, kneeling, rising vp, bowing and standing tovvardes ech other, the Sisters shall alwayes obserue the custome of the Friar-Minors, except in some Ceremonies which are not conuenient for them.

5. Furthermore no sister that can reade (of what condition soeuer she be) shall be excused from the Quire, eyther by night or day, but all the sisters are bound to come vnto Masse, and vnto all the Canonicall houres, excepting those who are sicke, or those who are

to ſerue them, vvith leaue of the Abbeſſe or her Vicareſſe, and thoſe who in the time of the Office ſhould be occupied in ſome common ſeruice of the Couent, vvith the knovvledge and leaue of the Abbeſſe: and therfore all the officers ought to haue ſuch forecaſt in their affayres and offices, that they diſpatch them in ſuch ſort as they may accompliſh the diuine office in the Quire with the others.

6. The ſiſters alſo who cãnot read and are not ſicke or imployed in the ſeruice of the others, ſhall likewiſe come to the Quire to fulfil the diuine office, vnto which they are bound, and that in ſome place aſſigned vnto them: and if the Abbeſſe or her Vicareſſe ſhould find any ſi-

ster negligēt in the aforsaid points, they may duely punish her, according to the quality of the offence.

7. Further we ordaine, that on the two dayes betweene the feast of S. Clare, and the Assumption of our Blessed Lady, they shall serue the feast of S. Clare with nine Lessons; the other dayes of the Octaue after the said feast, they shall make a commemoration of S. Clare at *Benedictus*, and *Magnificat*: the Octaue day being the feast of S. *Ludouicus*, which is *Duplex maius*, they shall make a Cōmemoration of S. Clare at both the Euensongs and Mattins.

8. Againe we ordaine, that in the time of a generall Interdict, the sisters conforme themselues vnto the principall Church of the towne, or

place

place where they reside when the said Interdict shall be lawfully signified vnto them, by those vnto whome it appertaineth, or by their certaine messengers or letters; and then the gates of their Church being shut, and the excommunicated being excluded, the sisters shall say all the diuine office as they say the Office of our B. Lady on simple feasts, not sitting but stãding, according to the custome: & if it should happen, that within the time of the said Interdict, any deputed to the seruice of the Couent, or any of the Sisters within should fall sicke, they shall communicate them; & if they should dye they shall be buried with a low voice, hauing in lik sort excluded forth those who are interdicted or excommunicated; so

neuer-

neuerthelesse, that nothing be o-mitted appertaining to the Office of the dead, or Communion.

9. And for as must as it is contained in the forme of life, that the Sisters who can reade shall say the Office of the dead, without expressing the day, houre, or by what manner or obligation they shall discharge it; such is the obscurity of the letter, as also the diuersity of opinions and writings vpon it, that I cannot giue any certaine resolution how they shall performe it; therfore to take away all ambiguity and difficulty which may arise in this point, to discharge their Consciences, and the more to succour and relieue the poore soules of the faithfull departed; I will & ordayne, that hence forward be done

done as we haue alwaies accustomed, to wit, that euery day all the Sisters say the Office of the Dead with one Nocturne and the Laudes, except the Thursday, Friday and Saturday of the Holy Weeke, & also when they reade the whole *Dirige* of three Nocturnes. The sisters who cānot read shal likwise euery day say the Office of the Dead with *Pater Nosters*, as is contained in the forme of life.

10. And for as much as prayer is necessary to goe forward in the seruice of God and make progresse in vertue, we ordaine that for this effect there be deputed for euery day two particuler houres, the one after Mattins, and the other after Euensong, with a quarter of an houre after Complin, for an

examine of Conſcience.

11. Alſo to keepe the body better ſubiect to the ſpirit, and in remẽbrance of the Paſſion, and eſpecially the moſt cruel flagellation of our Bleſſed Sauiour; we likewiſe ordaine that the Siſters take diſcipline, three a week in Aduẽt & Lẽt, & two a week the reſt of the yeare: which, with the aboue mentioned point of prayer, we will ſtill haue obſerued, vnles for ſome occaſion it be for a time omitted, which is left to the diſcretiõ of the Abbeſſe: but if it should be for any long ſpace, she is bound to aske the counſell of the Diſcreet.

Of

Of Abstinence.

CHAP. IIII.

FOR so much as it is contained in the forme of life, that the Sisters ought to fast at all times; vve say consequently, that they ought to abstaine at all times and in all places from eating flesh. And although in the forme of life be contained this clause; to wit, that on Christmas day, on what day soeuer it falleth, the Sisters may mak two refectiō; we declare that therby it is not graunted vnto them, that on the said day they may eate flesh, no more then on al Sundaies, on which the Sisters may also al in common make two refections, as all Christians doe on the Sundaies of Lent, according to the custome and ordinance of our holy Mother the Church.

2. It is also contained in the same forme of life, that with the young, & weake the Abbesse shall mercifully dispēce as she thinketh good; whereupon it is to be noted, that in this dispensation one cannot commonly well determine the necessity of the age, or weaknes, sith it happeneth oftentimes, that some are more strong at 13. yeares, then others at 16. and some also more grieued and weakned with a short and light sicknes, then others are vvith a grieuous and long sicknes; for which cause we exhort them all in our Lord, that

in

in all things they carry themselues so prudently, that amongst them doe more shine the charity of Iesus Christ, then ouer great & indiscreet austerity: in such sort neuertheles, that the Abbesse also doe not to easily dispense without true necessity, because by such dispensatiōs many times there haue come great relaxatiōs in some Religions.

5. The Abbesse neuerthelesse, or her Vicaresse, by the counsell of the discreet may dispense with the young, sicke, and weake, that they may take their refection oftentimes in a day, when true and iust necessity requireth it, for whome also they shall sufficiently prouide in their necessityes or weaknes, as well in meate as in other thinges.

4. Further we ordaine that the Abbesse haue diligēt care, that with the almes which come vnto her, she prouide competently for the Sisters in common, according to to quantity of almes, to the end that the sisters haue not occasion to desist, and giue ouer their vertuous beginings, and holy exercises, for want of common, or sufficient refections.

Of Confession, and of Communion: of the Confessour and his Companions.

CHAP. V.

TO the end that amongst the Sisters of this Order purity of hart & body may haue vigour,

gour, and be nourished, and that the loue and deuotion, vnto the most holy Body of our Lord, be alwaies augmented and increased: we will and ordaine, that aboue, the number mentioned in their forme of life (to wit that the Sisters with leaue of the Abbesse doe confesse twelue times in the yeare) euery Sister who shall not be lawfully hindred, may confesse twice euery weeke, and likewise as often (besides the seauen times written in the forme of life) shall receaue with the greatest deuotion they are able, the pretious Body of our Lord, in the Conuentuall Masse, except with leaue of the Abbesse or the counsaile of the Confessour of the Couent, any would deferre or abstaine from the said communion vntill another day, for some iust cause; admonishing them strictly to haue a great and particular care, that they doe it with the best preparation, and greatest reuerence they shall be able, to the end they doe not vndertake so great a work through custome, but with feruour of spirit.

2. Likewise we will, and also commaund by Obedience, that no Sister (of what condition so euer she be) may presume, to confesse to any Confessour, Religious, or secular of what degree, condition, or dignity soeuer he be, vnder coulour of any grace, or priuiledge graunted to the one, or other, then vnto the Confessour of the Couent, except the Abbesse by the counsaile of the greatest part of the dis-

discreet sisters, & that for iust & resonable cause, giue leaue vnto her.

3. Againe we ordaine, that after the last peale is rung vnto Compline, vntill after Tierce, no Sister may go to Confession without necessity.

4. And notvvithstanding, that in the forme of life it be contained, that it is lawfull for the Chapline, to celebrate Masse within the monastery, to communicate the sicke Sisters; neuerthelesse for many perils, daungers, and inconueniences, that heer by might ariue vnto the Sisters; we commaund all Abbesses and Portresses and all others present and to come of euery place, and Couent, that they neuer permit any Priest, Relicous, or Secular, to celebrate with

in their Cloister, or to Communicate either sicke, or sound, except any of them vvere oppressed vvith some grieuous sicknes, or long contagious disease, through which she could not, or it were not conuenient, for some great daunger, that she should come to Masse, or receaue the body of our Lord with the others in the Church: then in such a case we grunt, that in the seauen tymes ordayned in the forme of life, and more often, if the Abbesse with the counsaile of the Discreet, do find it conuenient, and for the consolation of the sicke, the Confessour with his Cõpanion, may, for this administration, enter within the Cloister.

5. Further, although it be contained in the sayd forme of life, that

that the Sisters shall haue mercifully a Chaplaine of the Order of the Friar-Minors, vvith a Clarke of good name, and discreet, and two lay Brothers, louers of holy conuersation and modesty, for ayde of their Pouerty; we declare that the sayd words ought to be vnderstood in the manner following: to wit, that the Sisters in euery couent haue, or may haue, if they haue need, foure Brothers of the Order of the Friar-Minors, of whome the first and principall, shall be a Priest their Chaplaine & Confessour, who ought to be pious, prudent, deuout and discreet, and well approued in Regular obseruance, not to young but of a conuenient age: the second shall be his companion, who must not only be a Clarke, but also a

Prieſt of good name, prudent and diſcreet, vnto whome the Confeſſour of the Siſters may confeſſe ſo often, as it is needfull: the other two ſhall be lay Brothers,& ought to be,as the forme of life ſaith, zelatours of holy conuerſation, and modeſty.

6. Which foure Brothers,the Abbeſſe of euery Couent ought by the coūſaile of the Diſcreet humbly to demaund, and require, of the grace and fauour of the Reuerend Father Miniſter-Generall, or of the Prouincialls, or their Vicars, and the ſaid ſayd miniſter Generall for all the Couents of the ſayd Siſters, or the Prouinciall-Miniſters, or their Vicars for the Couents which are ſcituated in their Prouinces & Vicaries, ought

merci-

mercifully, in regard of the piety of our Lord, and of S. Francis, to condescend vnto their said Postulation and request, and to giue them the said foure Brethren, or at the least a Father with his companion, in the Couents, where the Abbesse & the Sisters haue no need of lay Brothers.

Of the obseruance of Cloister.

CHAP. VI.

POPE Innocent the forth hath declared that those who haue vowed to keep this Rule and manner of life, ought to keep, and obserue perpetuall Cloister; and that it shall be no more lawfull, and that there be not giuen vnto them licence or power in all the time of their life to goe forth of the inclosure of their Monastery, vnles it were to build or to plant this Religion, or to reforme it in some monastery, or to take vpon them the gouernement or correction therof, or for to shunne some other great danger; and that then it be with the licence of the minister Generall, of the order of the Friar-Minors, or of the Prouinciall of the Prouince, or of their Vicars wherin the said monastery shall be scituated.

2. And when it doth hapen that they do send any Sisters forth of their monastery for the aforesaid causes; we will, and ordaine that they be accompanyed vvith honest persons, and fearing God, and

and that they goe vnto the other Couent assigned for them, with all speed possible.

3. Those who in this sort shalbe transported, must be carefull when they are amongst the secular, to shun all vaine and vndecent words or lookes, or full beholding of any one, but that they shew themselues mortifyed, speaking humbly, and conuersing modestly, with euery one, as it beseemeth the handmaydes of Iesus Christ, and the daughters of S. Clare.

4. In like manner because in the forme of life mention is made of Sisters seruing without the monastery, who make profession as the other Sisters, as it is there written (except the vow of Cloister) and goe in and out, and serue the

other

other Sisters, of thinges necessary to be done without the monastery as it is expedient; neuertheles, for many perils, and dangers which by this occasion might come vnto the said Sisters, and their Couents, Pope Bennet the tweluth hath or-ordained, and instituted, that from hence forward no Sister Professed presume to goe forth of the Cloister, except for the causes mentioned in the forme of life: we likewise willing that the said ordinance should be inuiolably obserued, doe command, that all the Sisters of what state and condition so euer they be, who are bound to the obseruance of the first Rule of Saint Clare, or shall heerafter be bound thereunto, that they alwayes perseuer vnder perpetuall Cloister, in such

ſuch ſort that hereafter none of thē haue faculty vnder the name of ſeruants, or for any other cauſe, to goe forth of the ſaid Cloiſter, except, as is ſayd, in the cauſes before ſpecifyed. Neuertheleſſe if in time to come the ſiſters ſhold haue need of the help, and ſeruice of ſome deuout women, which are modeſt and diſcreet, and well aged, they may receaue them vnto their help and ſeruice, ſo notwithſtanding as they in no ſort enter within the monaſtery.

5. Further we ordaine, that in euery Couent there be made in an opē & cōmon place, one only ſtrōg Wheele, of a conuenient height & largenes, and ſo compaſſed, that by no clefts or creuiſſes, any one may ſee into the Couent from without,

nor

nor from within forth of the same; by which Wheele the Sisters may receaue the thinges that shall be brought vnto them, and giue forth that which is to be giuen forth: but if the said thinges were so great and so long that they could not be giuen in or out by the wheele, they shall be giuen by the gate, into the monastery, and forth by the same, when it is expedient.

6. In like manner for the more surety & purity of the Sisters and Couents, we ordaine, that in no Couent made, or heerafter to be made of this Order, there be by any meanes permitted to be made, other Wheele, Gate, or Speak-house then the accustomed: wherfore it sufficeth that in euery Couent, and at all times, there be one only

only Speak-house, with a Wheele, and one Grate, and one Gate, and that in a common and publike place.

7. Againe we ordaine, that by the Wheele be made the Speak-window, garnished vvith a strong grate of iron, at which grate the Sisters shall speake when it is needful, according to the manner set down in the forme of life, & in these present Ordinances, for iust occasions.

8. In like sort we ordaine, that within the inclosure of the Couent, right ouer against the Principall Gate, there be another Gate vvhich shall in such sort be placed, that the Sisters by no meanes be able to approach, or goe vnto the principall Gate, and that none from without, by reason of the second

second gate, be able to see into the Couêt, through an creuisses, if there should chance to be any in the first gate, nor heare the Sisters frō within. Likwise we will, that the gardē dore, and the dormitory be strongly locked in the night.

9. For greater surety of the sayd Sisters we ordayne, that no Sister of what condition so euer she be, put letter of commendation, or any other writing, eyther open, or shut, either by herself, or by others, at the Wheele, Grate, nor Gate, neyther cause any to be there layd, to the end of being sent or carryed forth: and whatsoeuer letter there put, or cast, or at any other part whatsoeuer, none shall presume to receaue, or cause to be receaued, nor open, or read, vntill the letter

hath

hath wholy bin presented vnto the Abbesse, which letters the Abbesse ought to reade before any Sister do receaue them, and if the Abbesse finde any thing in the said letters vnfit, they shall in no sort be giuen vnto the Sister to whome they are sent, or by whō they were sent forth of the Couent, but the Sister shall be grieuously punished, and none shall be permitted to put their letters into the hands of those who should carry them.

10. In like manner, that no Abbesse doe read any letter, which is sent vnto her from without, nor doe send any forth of the Monastery to any person vntill the letter haue byn presented to one of the Discreete Sisters assigned for this effect by the other Discreet, which

sister ought to be changed euery yeare, and another ordained and assigned in her place: which sister thus assigned ought to reade all the letters before the Abbesse do reade thē, or send thē forth of the couent.

Of the election of the Abbesse, Discreete, and the other Officers.

CHAP. VII.

NOTWITHSTANDING that the Rule say, That the Sisters shall procure spedily the Minister Generall, or the Prouinciall of the Friar-Minors, who may with the word of God, exhort them vnto concorde, and vnion, and to seeke the common profit,

profit, in the election of the Abbesse; we neuertheles, considering the many affaires of the Superiors, as also the continuall occupations of the sayd Generall and Prouinciall, in respect of the gouernement and care of their subiects; for these and many other iust reasons, ordaine, that they being hindred by any busines, may giue charge vnto any other Father whome they shall iudge sufficient for that affaire.

2. To the end that in this election the sisters may proceed more securely, we will and ordaine, that when the Abbesse of any Couent shall be departed forth of this life, or detayned with any long infirmity, in such sort that she could not well exercise her office, or that she for some iust and reasonable cause,

would renounce the ſaid Office, or that ſhe were a violator of the Rule and holy Obſeruance, or found culpable in any enormous crime, or hainous offence, preſently three dayes after her death, depoſing, or abſolution, the profeſſed Siſters ought to prouide thẽſelues of another Abbeſſe, by Canonicall Election: in which Election none ought to be choſen for Abbeſſe, if ſhe be not 30. yeares of age, & haue expreſly vowed the forme of life, and bin well tryed therin.

3. When they haue that election to make, they ſhall hold this order. Firſt the 3. day after her death, the Vicareſſe ſhall certify the Superiour who then reſideth in the Prouince, by a letter or meſſenger of the death, or depoſition of

of their Abbesse, beseeching him to come, or to send one to make the Election of another Abbesse; and in the meane time whilest they expect his comming, the Sisters shall make continuall & feruent prayer vnto Almighty God, beseeching him to dispose all things to the honour and glory of his diuine maiesty.

4. We command by holsome Obedience, that the Sisters doe not speake vnto ech other about the election, as it were to cou̅saile, or say, It seemeth vnto me that such a one is fit, or, What do you thinke of such a one; but that euery one doe leaue the affaire vnto the inspiratiō of the holy Ghost, and that they take great heede in all their elections to proceed purely,

ly, ſincerely, holilv , and Canonically, without cauillation; and that being altogeather vnited in peace and charity, they chooſe her whom they know to be fitteſt for the ſaluatiō of ſoules, & profit of the monaſtery.

5. To the end that the Siſters may be more vnited & conformed vnto the diuine will, and may the better know it, the ſame morning the Election is to be made, the Siſters ſhall communicate if it be poſſible, and the ſame morning alſo Maſſe ſhall be ſayd of the holy Ghoſt. And note that the Vicareſſe ought to write, or cauſe to be written all in one hand, two or three times, as many bills in number, as there are Siſters profeſſed, vvherein theſe vvordes ſhall be

written,

written. I choose for our Reuerend Mother Abbesse Sister N. and the Vicaresse shall giue vnto euery Sister one of the said bils, wherein euery Sister shall write the name of her whome she iudgeth according vnto God and conscience, to be the fittest to exercise that office. When the Superiour or Visitour, or he who shal be assigned to make the said Election, shal be entred into the Chapter-house, al the Sisters being there assembled, he shal mak them an exhortation concerning the election: that being done, all the Sisters shall depart out of the Chapter-house, and returne one by one to the Superiour, giuing him their bill, wherin they haue written the name of her whome they choose: & hauing all deliuered their bils, they ſhall agayne al togeather enter into the Chapter-houſe, and the Prelate who hath receaued the bils ſhall pronounce the voyces, begining with her who hath the feweſt, vntill they be all ended, and ſhe who ſhall be found to haue the moſt voyces (more then the halfe) ſhalbe truly elected. And if peraduenture ſhe ſhould not be elected at the firſt, they ſhall againe returne vnto the election, in the ſame manner, vntill ſhe be choſen: and thus in euery Election, it is neceſſary, and it ſufficeth, to haue more then halfe the voices: She being choſen, and the voices pronounced by the Superiour, he ſhall confirme her in the name of the Father, of the Sonne, and of the Holy Ghoſt, Amē. That being done they

they shall say, *Te Deum Laudamus*: and at the end the Prelate sayth, *Confirma hoc Deus*, and the prayer *Actiones*: & after all the Religious shall go & imbrace their new Mother, & shall acknowledge her for their true, and lawfull Abbesse, and Superiour.

6. The same manner ought to be held in the election of the Vicaresse, and all other Officers, excepting that they shall only name thē by voices without writing any thing. And to the end that peace, loue. & truth of good conscience may alwaies remaine amongst the said Sisters, we admonish thē in our Lord Iesus Christ, that in all their elections, mutations, & changing of the officers and discreet, they shunne all ambitions, discordes,

malice, and euill affection, in promoting the vnfittest, and deposing the worthiest and most sufficient, for therby they should hurt their one consciences very much.

8. Contrariwise that none of them being chosen by the will of the holy Ghost, & voyce of the Sisters, vnto any Office, do refuse the paine and labour; but that for the loue of our Lord, they humbly accept it, and exercise it with diligence, according to the grace which God shall giue them; and that they doe not demand to be absolued or deposed from their office, without great, and reasonable cause, and by sound and good counsaile; and that in exercising their office they alwaies haue good patience, and charitable sufferance: for he, for

whose

whose loue they doe it, will giue and distribute vnto them, euerlasting reward.

The manner to hould Chapter.

CHAP. VIII.

FOR so much as according to the forme of life, the Abbesse is bound to call her Sisters vnto Chapter at least once a weeke: to the end that this may be euery where and alwaies obserued, we appoint and ordaine, that the Abbesse, or Vicaresse be carefull to assigne such an houre to hold the said Chapter, that all the Sisters in health may come vnto it. Besides which Chapter, there may be added, one or two, euery weeke according to the number of Sisters,

and

and diuersity of affayres; and for this, there shall be nothing omitted of the diuine Office, or of the other common offices.

2. As often as the Abbesse vvould gather her Sisters vnto Chapter, the bel of Obedience shal be only tolled, and then all the Sisters in health who are not for that present necessarily occupyed, or in the seruice of the sicke, shall be bound so soone as they heere the signe of the bell, to come vnto all the assemblies.

3. The Abbesse or Vicaresse, after the inuocation of the holy Ghost, shall make the generall recommendations for the liuing and the dead, naming in particular the benefactours which haue bestowed any almes vpon them: which

recom-

recommendations being made, the Sisters rise vp, saying the suffrages for thē, to wit, *Ad te leuaui occulos meos. De profundis clamaui*, with the suffrages which follow, *Pater noster*, ℣. *Et ne nos*. ℟. *Sed libera* ℣. *Fiat pax &c.* and at the end they shall say *Pater noster*, & the Abbesse, *Deus det nobis suam pacem. Amen.*

4. Then the Abbesse and all the Sisters doe againe sit downe, and if there be Nouices they must first speake their fault, and hauing receaued pennance of the Abbesse or her Vicaresse, depart forth of the Chapter, and goe into the Church, and pray for the other.

5. They being departed, all the professed togeather shall prostrate themselues, and speake their faults

faults in generall, and for the same receaue generall pennance: and after that, euery one in particular shall acknowledge their fault humbly, and deuoutly, as they find themselues to haue fayled, & that with ioyned hands, and vpon their knees, prostrate on the ground, beginning at the yongest: & then the Abbesse, or her Vicaresse doth impose them pennance, euery one according to the greatnes of the fault committed; and if it be needfull she doth admonish, reprehend, and correct them charitably, as she shall thinke expedient, without shewing any partiality: & the Sisters ought always to receaue the sayd pennance, with all humility and patience, & accomplish it with deuotion.

6. And

6. And let all the Sisters, take very great heede, that they neuer make any Reply in Chapter, or els where, or any couered excuse; and that none be so bolde as to speake there, without the leaue of the Abbesse.

7. Let the Sisters take likewise heed, that they do in no sort vpraide ech other of the faults corrected in Chapter, or Visitation, nor any other defectes committed in the world and if heerein any one should be found faulty, she shalbe seuerely punished by the Abbesse.

8. All things then being accoplished & finished, as hath byn sayd, if they haue any busines to treate of according to the forme of life, they may speake therof togeather, and

that

that with expedient & due grauity, & modesty, taking carefully heed to themselues, that they doe not there speake, or vtter any disordinate, superfluous, or vnprofitable wordes: and all thinges thus accōplished, the Abbesse making the signe of the Crosse, sayth: *Adiutorium nostrum in nomine Domini.* ℟. *Qui fecit &c.* and so they depart forth of Chapter, in the name of our Lord.

Of silence, and the manner of speaking at the Speake-house, and at the Grate.

CHAP. IX.

FOR as much as peace is the worke of Iustice, and silence the gard and keeper of the said peace, to the end that the feruour of deuotion, grow not cold, and be not extinguished by disordinate & ouer much talke, we ordaine that the Sisters keepe silence as it is contayned in the forme of life, to wit from after Compline, vntill Tierce of the next morning be read.

2. They shall keep continuall silence as the forme of life saith, in the

the Church, Dormitory, and in the Refectory when they eate, except in the Infirmary.

3. And although in the ſayd forme of life their be no mention made, that they ſhall keep ſilence in the Cloiſter; the reaſon may be that in the time of S. Clare when S. Francis gaue her the forme of life in the monaſtery of S. Damian, where ſhe remained, they had then no Cloiſter, by reaſon of the great pouerty of the place: we neuertheles diligently cōſidering that Pope Gregory the ninth ordained, in the firſt Rule, that the ſayd Siſters, should keep continuall ſilence, at all times, and in all places, and likewiſe becauſe in all Religions well ordered the Cloiſter is the firſt place next vnto the Church, where they

they are accuſtomed to keep ſilence; we inſtitute, and ordaine, that from hence forward all the Siſters keepe alwayes ſilence, in the Cloiſter, as in the other place, named in the forme of life.

4. Further we command, that no Siſter of what office degree or condition ſoeuer she be, doe goe vnto the Speake-houſe without licence of the Abbeſſe or her Vicareſſe, and alſo that no Siſter hauing leaue to go vnto it in any ſort, ſpeak to any perſon at the ſayd Speake-houſe, except there be preſent two profeſſed Siſters plainly hearing & vnderſtanding that which they ſay; and they muſt be of the number of the eight Diſcreet of the Couent. For ſeeing that at the grate in the Church where they are in the preſence

ſence of Almighty God, and his Angels, there muſt be three of the ſaid Diſcreet aſſigned; how much greater reaſon is there, that the Speake-houſe which is a more cōmon and publike place, there ſhould be two of the number of the ſayd Diſcreet aſſigned vnto that Siſter, who ought to ſpeake, hauing leaue of the Abbeſſe, for any reaſonable cauſe.

5. Likewiſe we ordaine, that no Siſter doe euer ſpeake at the Gate of the Couent, with any perſon from without, neither aloud nor ſoftly, nor with her companions, or without them.

6. Further we wil & ordaine, that when any Siſter for any euident profit or neceſſity, or for any reaſonable cauſe, ought to ſpeake at

at the Grate which is in the Church vnto any person, before and after she beginneth to speake, one therunto appointed may a little hold vp the Curtine, which hangeth within, and presently to let it fall downe againe in the accustomed place, in such sort that whē she speaketh, she be neuer seene by any person in the face, & no Sister shall speake there except as the forme of life saith, vnto persons of accoūt which are mature and modest, or their neerest Parents & kindred or spirituall friendes, and that very seldome.

7. If it shold happē that any person were to enter in & speake with them, they shall couer modestly their faces, and decline a little, as it appertaineth vnto the modesty of

of Religion.

8. Furthermore in S. Martins Lent (which we will haue to begin the day after all-Saints day, and to last vnto the Natiuity of our Lord) & in the great Lent (which we will haue to begin the day after *Quinquagesima*, and last vntill Easter) that no Sister within these tymes speake at the speake-house, or at the grate vnto any person, except (for the causes contayned in the forme of life) the Abbesse, or her Vicaresse, & the Portresse only, for the profitable busines of the Couent, as vnto this present, it hath bin accustomed.

9. In like manner, within this time no Sister shall write vnto her Parents, or friendes, except it be vpon some extraordinary occasion,

ſion, that cannot be deferred, the which ſhall be committed vnto the diſcretion of the Abbeſſe.

10. Againe we exhort them in our Lord Ieſus Chriſt that when any Siſter doth ſpeake at the grate in the Church, or at that in the Speake-houſe (for at the wheele it may not be permitted) that ſhe take heed of prolixe, vayne, vnprofitable, and worldly wordes, but that the wordes which proceede from their mouth, be holy, modeſt, and profitable, as beſeemeth the handmaides of our Lord Ieſus, and the obſeruers of the holy Ghoſpell.

11. To ſhun the ſuſpitions & familiarities of ſecular perſons, and their long and vnprofitable diſcourſes, we ordaine that the Siſters

be in no ſort God-mothers vnto any man or vvoman Child, by themſelues, or by any perſon interpoſed.

22. Further we ordaine, that when it is needfull for any to enter into the Cloiſter, either to viſite the ſick, or for any other iuſt cauſe, the Siſters vvhich haue leaue to ſpeake, ſhall not ſpeake vnto them but in the preſence of two Siſters, which muſt heare them, and they muſt be of the number of the diſcreet, & aſſigned by the Abbeſſe or her Vicareſſe, for this effect.

Of

Of the obseruance of Pouerty; and that the Sisters may not admit any possessions, nor haue any thing proper.

CHAP. X.

FOR so much as according to the forme of life, the Abbesse, and all the Sisters, are bound to obserue Pouerty, which they haue promised vnto God and vnto S. Francis, to wit, not receauing or hauing possessions, or propriety, by themselues, or by any person interposed; to the end they may obserue the sayd pouerty, more perfectly and intierly in not receauing or detayning any possessions, or

 proprie-

propriety; we forbid by obedience the said Sisters, in any sort to receaue any house to hire, or land, or garden to plough, or medow to till or vineyard, or any other thing, to manure, or possesse.

2. Furthermore they shall not haue inheritances or rents, nor shal not receaue yearly prouisions, or perpetuall almes eyther by themselues, or by any other person interposed. Likwise not to haue granaries, or cellers so full of thinges bought or begged, or otherwise gained, in so great plenty and aboundance, that they should sell of the said prouision, or be therewith able to passe their life a whole yeare, without begging: this doth wholy repugne vnto their pouerty.

3. They

3. They ſhall alſo neuer haue oxen, kyne, or flocks of ſheep, or ſtable of horſes, nor cuppes or diſhes of gold, or ſiluer, or any other pretious thinges: likewiſe Ievvelis of gold, or ſiluer, or money, or pretious ſtones, or any other thinges, or prouiſions vvhich may laſt aboue a yeare: all theſe are prohibited vnto them.

4. Furthermore we wil, that in all their garments, aparell, veſſells, furniture, and in all thinges as well of the Church as otherwiſe, they ſhunne all curioſity, and ſuperfluity, to the end that in them alwaies may ſhine the holy pouerty, and amongſt thē euer raigne the neceſſity and ſpare vſe of thinges, as it appertaineth vnto thoſe who ought to follow the moſt holy Pouerty.

5. Fur-

5. Further we will and ordaine, that with the thinges which are giuen vnto the Sisters in Wills, or Testaments they do in such sort as Pope Nicolas the third hath ordained, in the declaration of the Rule of the Friar-Minors.

6. Againe, seing that the forme of life saith, that the Sisters shall appropriat nothing to themselues, neither house, nor place, nor any other thing. And by the said Pope Nicolas the third, and Clement the fifth, and many other most holy Fathers, it hath bin declared in the declarations of the Rule of the Friar-Minors, that the renuntiation and abandoning of all thinges, which the said Brothers do make, ought to be vnderstood and obserued aswell in particular, as in common

mon; and we in this article adhering vnto the aforesaid writing, *will and command* the said abandoning, and renuntiation of the propriety of all thinges, which the Sisters do make for the loue of God (as meritorious, and profitable, & worthy of eternall retribution) to be entierly & inuiolably obserued of all the said Sisters present, and to come, as well in particular as in common: neuertheles the said Sisters may, with a safe conscience, haue the bare vse of al things, which are graūted according to the forme of life, and of those which are not therin forbiddē them, without the propriety of them, as the vse of thinges necessary for the celebration and vpholding of the diuine office.

7. For

7. For the habitation and nourishment of the body, and for the execution of the offices, and affaires which are necessary vnto thē according to the said forme of life, and their holy Religion, they may also haue the vse of such thinges as are freely giuen or procured them for Gods sake; and likewise of those which they haue gained by the labour of their handes; since those things which are giuen, begged, or gained doe not repugne vnto pouerty.

8. Further we ordaine, that the Almes or thinges giuen in particular, or sent vnto the Sisters shall be distributed, in particular, or in cōmon vnto those who haue need according to the discretion of the Abbesse; and we will not haue it to be law-

lawfull for any Sister, to giue that which is sent vnto her, or giuen her by her parēts or friends, vnto any other needy Sister, or to send it to any other person forth of the Co-uent, without the liking & expresse leaue of the Abbesse.

9. Further we will, that concerning the debtes which are to be made, that the Sisters do alwayes, and in all times, as it is contained in the forme of life.

10. Againe, we command thē to take great heede not to make stately & sumptuous buildings, but that they content themselues with those which are meane & humble.

Of the Sicke Sisters.

CHAP. XI.

VVE ordaine, that vvhen any Sister shall be grieuously sicke, or very weake, the Abbesse or her Vicaresse shall be bound presently to prouide her of conuenient seruice: and the Sisters which are deputed to serue the sicke shall take great heede that they doe not commit any notable defect in their offices, but that they serue them humbly, deuoutly & in feruour of charity, euen as they would be serued, if themselues were sicke.

2. Likewise the Abbesse if she be

be not lawfully hindred, ſhall be bound at the leaſt once euery day, to viſit the ſicke Siſters, and in her abſence the Vicareſſe is bound to doe it, to the end that by their negligence the ſicke Siſters doe not want any thing in their ſicknes.

3. The Abbeſſe and her Vicareſſe, ſhall take heed that they doe not aſke Counſell for the recouery, and health of the ſicke Siſters of any Phiſitian, or Surgeon, which is not a Catholike, and they ſhall always ſend for remedy vnto the deuouteſt, which are to be found, but they ſhall let none of them to enter into the Cloiſter, but for iuſt neceſſity, and ſicknes, and thoſe who are to enter ſhall be alwayes duely accompanied, in ſuch ſort, that the Abbeſſe, or her Vicareſſe,

or two or three Discreet of the Couent, be alwaies present, vntill they be departed forth of the Cloister.

4. Againe, if it should happen that any Sister, or many should be sick of any grieuous disease, as the Leprosy, or any weaknes of head, or lightnes of vnderstanding, or for other such like sicknesses, for which they could not conueniently remaine with the others, there shalbe prouided for them a chamber a part, within the Couent, and for their conuenient seruice as their sicknes doth require, in such sort that none do euer goe forth of the Cloister.

5. Further, we exhort in our Lord all the Sisters present and to come, that for the loue of God, & for the bitter death and passion of

our Sauiour Iesus Christ, they will not loath or disdayne to serue those who shall be so sicke, but that humbly and deuoutly as it shall be needfull, they exhibit vnto them, all humanity, and charitable seruice.

6. If the Abbesse, or her Vicaresse, or the other Sisters deputed vnto the seruice of the sicke, do not prouide for them according to their condition, and quality, & according to the possibility of the place, in counsaile, in meate, and other thinges necessary, they shall be accused by all the other Sisters vnto the Visitour in the time of visitation, & be grieuously punished, as cruell, if they commit any notable default in the seruice of the said sicke.

7. It is alſo contained in the forme of life, to wit according to Pope Innocent the fourth, that the Siſters which are ſicke not of any long or grieuous ſicknesse, ſhall lye vpon ſackes filled with chaffe, and ſhall haue a cuſhion of feathers vnder their heads; but if peraduenture there were ſome ſicke, of any grieuous, or long ſicknes, or for any other reaſonable, and lawfull cauſe that they could not reſt vpon the ſayd chaffe-beds, it behoooueth otherwiſe to prouide for them, according vnto God and the counſaile of the Diſcreet; and therfore we will and ordayne that when it ſhall happen that any, or many ſicke of ſuch a ſicknes, the Abbeſſe, or her Vicareſſe doe prouide, or cauſe to be prouided with the

the counsell of the Discreete, fea-ther-beddes, for the said sicke, and other thinges necessary for them to rest vpon, according to the forme of life, & also as they in their conscience shall thinke it to be needful, and as the infirmity of the said sick doth require; and they shall cause them to rest vpon the said beddes with al humanity, as it shal be expedient vnto their infirmity.

8. The Abbesse also, or her Vicaresse, or the other Sisters deputed vnto the seruice of the sicke, shall diligently prouide, that when any depart forth of this life, at the time of her departure she shalbe cloathed with the Habit of the Order, and girded with the Cord, and the Vaile vpon her head, and shall be buryed so cloathed.

9. Againe it is contained in the forme of life, that those who haue neede of wollen sockes, may vse them; the which words are dispensatory, when necessity doth require it: and therfore we ordaine that no Sister of what office or condition soeuer she be, in time of health, weare socks, if she haue not actuall necessity; the which necessity is not to be determined according to the iudgment of euery Sister, but by the Abbesse with the counsaile of of the Discreet, or of the greatest part of them; which Abbesse when she shall see some stand in neede of sockes, or that they doe request her to dispense with them, then if it seeme needfull vnto the Abbesse, and the Discreet, and that there be manifest necessity, the conditions

of

of the party prudently considered, & the diuersity of times & places, she shall dispense with them, to weare wollen sockes, during the time of the said necessity; and if greater necessity should arise, she may also dispense with them, to weare leather soles vvith wollen sockes.

Of the manuall workes of the Sisters.

CHAP. XII.

FOr so much as the forme of life saith, that the Sisters vnto whō God hath giuen the grace of vvorking, shall worke after the Tierce; to the end that this may be better obſerued of al the Siſters, we will, that for the loue of God they doe not refuſe the offices of charity, and humility, but when the Abbeſſe or her Vicareſſe ſhall haue inioyned them any of the ſaid offices, for the common, or particular profit of the Couent, they ſhall receaue it willingly & ſweetly, without any murmuration or contradiction, and with great diligence they ſhal accompliſh it faithfully and deuoutly, as it hath byn commanded them.

2. When in the foreſayd manner, by the Abbeſſe, or her Vicareſſe, any of the forſaid things ſhall be inioyned, none of them being ſound of body and vnderſtanding, ſhall couer themſelues with the cloake of negligence, or

ſlouth-

slouthfulnes, or pride, in saying, God hath not giuen me the grace to doe such and such a worke: but they shal be humble and obedient, as it beseemeth those who haue vowed intiere obedience to the wil of those who doe command them.

3. The Abbesse, and her Vicaresse ought to take great heed, that they doe not command them any thing, which they know probably, or manifestly, that they could not, or are not able to doe.

4. Although in the said forme of life it be said, that the Sisters shal worke after the Tierce; we neuertheles considering the straite pouerty of the said Sisters, and the necessity and want which they may haue, graunt that if there should be in the Couent, any necessary or

conuenient worke to be done before the ſaid houre, that the Abbeſſe or her Vicareſſe, may command thoſe whome they thinke good to doe the ſaid workes, or to finiſh them, if they be begun.

5. Againe we command the ſaid Siſters that none of them from hence forward preſume, to make, or to finiſh any worke for their Order, or for any other perſon of what condition ſoeuer, or in what ſort ſoeuer, by which iuſtly they might be noted of vanity & curioſity; when it is needfull for the Siſters to doe any ſuch worke, before it be accepted, or begun, it ſhall be wholy preſented vnto the Abbeſſe, or her Vicareſſe, who ought to iudge whether the worke be fit to be done by the Siſters or not, &

nothing

nothing shall be done without her liking, or permission: and the Sisters which shall doe the contrary, shall be punished according to the discretion of the Abbesse or Vicaresse.

6. Againe, after the Masse, at a conuenient tyme, they may ring vnto worke, & then all the Sisters which haue no lawfull excuse, shal come to do the worke which is appointed, and enioyned them.

7. Furthermore, we ordaine, that all the Sisters present and to come, do alwayes, and in all places abstaine from all secular, & vaine pastimes, and from all worldly vaine playes of what thing, or in what sort soeuer they be.

8. When two, or many, are togeather, if they haue leaue to

ſpeake, and recreate (for otherwiſe they muſt keep ſilence) they ſhall ſpeake alwaies of God, and of the liues of Saints eyther liuing or dead, or of ſomthing belonging to the health of their ſoules, or of ſome decent and profitable buſines, and that they take great heed of all idle, hurtfull, and diſſolute wordes, as it becometh the handmaides of Ieſus Chriſt, and obſeruers of the holy Ghoſpell, and the profeſſours of holy Religion.

9. Further, vve forbid the Siſters to haue or keep in their Couent, or to reade, or write, or cauſe to be written, any Bookes wherein there ſhould be expreſly contained any open, or ſecret vanity, or carnality, or hiſtory of worldly perſons: neuertheles it is

law-

lawfull for them , to haue holy bookes in their Couents in common for the comfort and profit of their soules, which they may read in particular, or in common, at the table, or in any other place, according to the will & appointment of the Abbesse.

Of the correction of the faulty.

CHAP. XIII.

VVE ordain, that in euery Couent, the Abbesse, or in her absence the Vicaresse, doe admonish and correct the Sisters humbly, and charitably, to the end that they doe not fall into the pitt of transgressi-

on,

on, for want of correction and admonition; so that the said Superiours keep (as is ordained in the said correction) true charity, and sweet humility.

2. They shall also take heed that vnder the colour of humility and sweetnes, they doe not giue the Sisters occasion of liberty and relaxation; and vnder the shadow of charity, nourish true carnality of the body, and cruelty to the soules; but they shall correct them all equally as it is expedient, without any difference, according to their faults.

3. If it should happen (which God forbid) any Sister had committed so great a crime, or enormous sinne, that she had put her soule in daunger of perdition, and her

her Order in infamy, & confusion, or if there were any so rebellious, incorrigible, or perseuerant in her malice, so that she would in no sort amend; for such there shall be made in euery Couent, a chamber of discipline, strong but humane, wherin she shall be put & kept for a certaine time with bread and water, as fifteene dayes, a moneth, a yeare, or perpetually, according as the offence doth require it, and according to the discretion of the Abbesse & the Discreet.

4. Againe if it should happen that any Sister should rebell against the Abbesse or Vicaresse, & should say vnto them any vndecent and iniurious words, she shall eate bread and water only, sitting on the ground before all the Sisters

ſters, the ſpace of a whole refection.

Of the Portreſſe, and entring into the Monaſtery.

CHAP. XIIII.

ALTHOVGH in the forme of life it be contained, that the Portreſſe shall keep her reſidence the day tyme, in an open Cell without a dore; we neuertheles for many iuſt occaſions moouing vs heere vnto, will not haue that this be now obligatory, nor that it be by any meanes obſerued; for although in the time of Saint Clare, it was decent and lawfull for the Siſters, neuertheles it might be now very hurtfull & perilous vnto them. 2. Ther-

2. Therefore we desiring to prouide for their security and decency, Ordaine that they obserue the manner following, to wit, that there be deputed a Sister, fearing God, to keepe the Gate of the Monastery, and the Speak-house, one who is moderate, of good manners, diligent, discreet, and of conuenient age, to the end that (as the forme of life saith) she may with word and deed edify those vnto whome she doth speake, or with whome she conuerseth.

3. There shall be assigned her, a fit companion by the Abbesse, with the counsell of the Discreet, who being as fit, or fitter then herselfe, shall in the time of sicknes, which the said Portresse might incur, in all thinges fulfill her office:

vnto which two Portresses there shall be assigned another Sister of the number of the eight Discreet (vvhich may be changed euery weeke, and another assigned in her place) to heare those who speak vnto the Sisters. For no Sister (as hath byn sayd) ought to speake vnto any person from without, except there be present two Sisters, of the number of the eight Discreet, who must heare them: which three Sisters when it ringeth shall come to the chamber wherein the Wheele and the Speak-window is placed, in such sort, that the one doe not speake without the other two, nor they without the third, but shal be all three togeather.

4. The principall Portresse only shall answere those who doe speake

ſpeak at the Grate, & the other two ſhall be preſent & heare her: and if it ſhould hapen that any one wold ſpeak vnto one of the other Siſters, ſhe or one of her companions ſhall goe aſke leaue of the Abbeſſe or her Vicareſſe to ſpeake, and hauing licence, ſhe who is called for, may ſpeake, ſo as there be preſent two Siſters of the number of the Diſcreet, the principall Portreſſe being alwayes one, if the neceſſity of ſome other affayre doe not hinder her.

5. Further we ordaine, that the ſaid Cell or Chamber be furniſhed with a dore of wood, which ſhall alwayes aſwell by day as by night be locked with two keyes, vvhen the Portreſſes are not within it: of which two keyes the Abbeſſe ſhall

keep one in the night, and the Portresse the other, and the third Sister which is assigned vnto the other two by weekes, shall keep by day the key which the Abbesse doth keep in the night: Within which Speak-house none of the portresses may enter without the other.

6. As for the entring of any into the Monastery, we command firmely, and strongly that no Abbesse, nor her Sisters, doe euer permit any person, Religious or secular, of what state or dignity soeuer he be, to enter into the monastery: and it is not lawfull for any person whatsoeuer, except leaue were giuen them of the Popes Holines, or of the Lord Cardinall Protector of the Order.

7. From this law of not en-

tring,

tring, are exempted Phisitians and Surgeons for iust necessity, or sicknes; those also who for fire, or any other ruine, or perill, or danger, or to doe any worke which could not be done vvithout the monastery. If any Cardinall wold enter into the monastery, he shalbe receaued with reuerence and deuotion, but they shall intreate him to enter with two or three only, of the modestest of his company.

8. Neuertheles no Sister sicke nor in health, shall speake vnto any of thē, but in the māner contained in the forme of life, and principally they shall take heede that those which haue leaue to enter, be such that those which see them enter, may be edified of their liues, manners, and wordes, and that there

be not giuen vnto any person iust occasion of scandall.

9. Againe we ordaine that whē any thing is brought vnto the Couent which could not conueniently enter in at the wheele, as a barrel of beere, or any such like thing: the Abbesse, or Portresse and her companions, shall take heede that the Gate do not stand any longer open then it is needfull, and they shall not permit the carriers or bearers of the said thinges, to enter into any other place of the couent, then only into the place situated betwixt the two Gates of the Couent or to other places, to which of necessity they must come to place the said thinges.

10. The Sisters shall take heed that none enter besides those who

are

are necessary, nor permit those that are entred to stay any longer then the worke requireth.

11. The other Sisters must take heed that they be not seene by them that enter, except those who are deputed by the Abbesse or her Vicaresse, and that those speake not with thẽ, but only as much as the necessity of the thinges requireth.

12. To the end, that this care of the Sisters not being seene, be the better practized, vvhen as those who are to enter need not come further eyther for the worke or the bringing of any thing, then the place betweene two Gates; we will haue them to obserue this mãner, to wit, that the Portresses open the first Gate within the Couent &

enter into that place to open the secōd, which is the principall gate of the Couent, the which they shall not set wide open as the other, but only vnlocke it with the two keyes and lift vp the iron barre which goeth ouerthwart, and presently withdrew themselues vvithin the second Gate, locking it with the two keyes: & then those which doe bring the said thinges may lift vp the latch, and enter into that place, and put the thinges there which they do bring, and presently goe forth latching the dore after them, & then the Portresses againe enter in and locke the said principall Gate with the two keyes; and and then order the thinges which are brought in as it is conuenient.

13. Furthermore it is contayned

ned in the forme of life, that the Gate shall neuer be left in the day without one to keep it. Vpō which we say, that for all surety it suffiseth, that the two Gates be strongly locked as is aforesaid. And after that, these following wordes are written, *VVhen it is necessary that any doe enter into the Monastery to doe any worke, that then the Abbesse shall appoint one to open the Gate only to those who are deputed to doe the sayd worke, and not vnto others.* Vpon which wordes we say, that the said Portresse, who according to the forme of life, ought to be modest and discreete with those which are assigned her for her cōpanions, ought to suffice to opē the Gate vnto those who are to enter in, to doe any worke, or for any ther reaſonable and iuſt occaſions ſo neuertheles that she open it with the leaue of the Abbeſſe, and the ſaid Portreſſe ſhall then take heed of long talke or wordes with them, except only ſo much as is needfull & conuenient for to do the worke, for which they entred: but if it be neceſſary, they may leade them modeſtly and diſcreetly vnto the ſayd vvorke, as it shall be needfull.

14. No Siſter of what condition ſoeuer she be, shal euer goe to ſee the workmen, or their worke except thoſe who are appointed by the Abbeſſe, for the profit of the thing which is to be done; and vvhen it is needfull in this ſort to goe vnto them, they shall neuer goe without ſure company of the

the discreet: and they shall alwaies be in an open and common place, and they shall not remaine longer with them, or vse more wordes thē are necessary to doe, or finish the said worke.

15. The Abbesse, and all the Sisters shall take great heed that they doe not cause those workes which they themselues could doe, to be done by strangers; and that they do not permit any workmen or others, who doe enter, of what condition soeuer they be, to eate within the Cloister.

16. Further we exhort all the Sisters in Christ Iesus our Lord, that they neuer be solicitous or importune to procure the benedictions of Abbesses and consecrations of Nunnes, but let them content them-

themselues with their holy Profession, for which (if they doe well obserue it) they shall receaue the Benediction of the soueraigne Bishop our Lord Iesus Christ.

17. Againe we ordaine, that when the Confessour and his companion enter into the Monastery, that they be cloathed with sacred vestements, to wit, with the Albe or Surplisse.

18. Further we ordaine for the diuersity and difference of this present time, from that wherin the forme of life was giuen, that from hence forward there be no Masse celebrated within the Monastery neyther for the liuing, or exequies of the dead. To make the graue it shall not be lawfull for any to enter, except one or two diggers, or

masons

masons which are modest and honest: and that only in the Couents where the Sisters cannot digge, & close the graue as it is requisite.

19. Againe to bury the Sisters, they shall let none enter into the Cloister, but the Confessour & his companion, or in the absence of his companion, another modest Brother: and the sayd buriall being ended, and accomplished, they shall presently depart forth of the Monastery.

Of the Visitatour.

CHAP. XV.

BEING so that the Rule of life setteth downe two things cōcerning the Visitature: the first that

that he ought alwaies to be of the Order of the Friar Minors; the second that this ought to be done by the will and commandment of the Lord Cardinal protectour: the first is yet to be obserued, but not the second, because when the Rule was first instituted, neyther the monasteries of Sisters, nor the Sisters thēselues were then wholy subiect vnto the obedience and gouernement of the Friar-Minors; yet notwithstanding afterwardes, for certaine and reasonabble causes the care and gouernement of them hath bin wholy, and in euery respect committed vnto the Generall and Prouinciall-Ministers of the Friar-Minors by Pope Innocent the fourth, and diuers other holy Bishops.

2. To the end that we may more conformably proceed in the same Order by making of our Visitations; we doe ordaine, that according to the aforesaid forme of life, the said Sisters haue alwaies their Visitour of the aboue named Order of Friar-Minors, who according to the statutes of the late rehearsed Pope Innocẽt the fourth, ought to be assigned and commanded by the licence and apointment of the General-Minister of the same order, or of the Prouinciall-Ministers within the limmits of their administration; which Visitour the Sisters ought humbly to aske, or cause to be asked for, of one of the aforesaid persons, that is to say, eyther of the Generall ouer all the Couents of the said Order, or of

the Prouincialls of the Couents of their Prouinces.

3. Moreouer, we doe prohibite and forbid, that the sayd Sisters doe demaund or receaue, any other for Visitour, then such a one who is well knowne and approued other Religious life, good manners and faith, as also that hath the zeale of God, and that he be an obseruer of his Rule, and louer of holy Pouerty, and of all modesty.

4. The said Visitatour is bound to visite all the Couentes which shall be committed to his charge, once a yeare, or more often, if it shall be thought necessary: as also when he shall for some reasonable and iust causes be required thereunto by the Abbesse, and other of the discreet Sisters.

5. Also

5. Alſo we doe Ordaine, that they neuer procure the Viſitour to enter the more inward parts of the Couent, without great neceſſity, and this, at the time when he holdeth his Viſit iuridicall & ordinary.

6. When he entreth within, to viſit the Monaſtery he muſt ſhew himſelfe ſuch a one in all his actions, that thereby others may be mooued from good to better, and more inflamed in the loue of God, and haue alwayes mutuall Charity amongſt themſelues. He ought alſo to haue his companion with him in an open conuenient place, & ſo neere vnto him that the one may well perceaue and ſee the other without any difficulty: and that he ſo diſpatch, that he ſtay no lon-

ger within the Cloiſter, then during the ending of his ſaid buſines of Viſitation, which ended he ſhall goe preſently forth of the monaſtery.

7. When he ſhall come to viſit any Couent, he ſhall procure that he end his Viſite in the ſpace of two or three naturall dayes: & before he beginneth the ſaid Viſit, it is requiſite that he make an Exhortation to the Siſters, if at leaſt he be prepared for it, concerning the viſit which he is to make: after this, that he reade their Rule, with this preſent Ordinance where it ſpeaketh of the manner of Viſitation: next after he is to command euery one and al the Siſters, in vertue of profitable Obedience, that they anſwere him in plaine, and

good sooth, whether they do know, any thing in those thinges wherof, and wherupon he is to make inquisition, wherunto euery one and all the Sisters are bound firmely to obay in all thinges belonging to the office of Visitation.

8. The Visitour may (if he so please, and thinke it conuenient) obserue this manner of speaking, to wit, that he speake to all, or to some togeather, or with one secretly, two other Sisters being in the place not far off in his presence, but not so neere as they may heare what is spoken; to the end that by all meanes integrity may be kept: and then the Sisters may come one by one to giue informations, if there be any thing to be informed.

9. If any be accused of any fault

of crime, then as well the names of the accusers, as of the accused shall be written, togeather with the faultes they be accused off: and the visit being ended, the Sisters shall all be called into the Chapter, and the faults of the accused Sisters shal be declared, and a proportionable pennance giuen vnto them, if the crimes can be lawfully, really, and iuridically proued by two of good name. Neuertheles audience shall not be denied vnto any, to the end that they may excuse themselues if they haue any lawful excusation eyther in part or in whole; but the accused Sisters shall not enquire after the names of those who did accuse them, neyther shall they by any meanes be reuealed vnto them except in case, that the accused,

would

would seeke to cleere herselfe of the crime wherof she is accused, & so should iuridically aske that the names of her accusers might be reuealed and knowne.

10. If it should happen that any one had falsely or vniustly accused another, and that this might be legitimately knowne, she shall sustaine all that which the accused Sister should haue sustained, if she had bin found faulty of that crime, wherof by the other she was accused. Neuertheles if some one Sister in any Couent did certainly know some Sisters who had grieuously transgressed, or were at that time in some grosse crime, which could not be well proued at that time; the said Sister who knoweth it, may & ought to informe the Visitour of

the Sister, and of the crime, in such manner as she knoweth it, to wit secretly; and in this case the Visitour may by no meanes, at any time reueale the name of the Sister who is the accuser, vnto her accused Sister.

11. If any thing shold at any time happen, which he of himself could not conueniently amend, he shall make relation of it vnto his soueraine Superiour, that by his Counsell and commaundment the sayd offence may be punished, according as it deserueth.

12. The Abbesse ought to be carefull, that the estate of the Monastery be not concealed, eyther by herselfe or by her Sisters from the knowledge of the Visitatour, in the obseruance of their Religion,

on, in vnity of mutuall Charity, which they al ought to haue togeather; for this should be no small sinne, but an offence worthy to be grieuously punished.

13. Wherefore, we will and cōmaund, that those thinges which are to be corrected, and amended according to the forme of life, eyther publikely, or secretly, they shall propose and declare vnto the Visitour in the best manner that they shall be able: & if any should doe otherwise, be she Abbesse or whosoeuer of the rest, she is to be punished seuerely by the Visitour, according as she hath deserued.

14. When the Visitatour shall make his Visit publickly or secretly; amongst other thinges which he should quire of the Si-

ſters, he ſhall firſt demaund of thinges moſt Eſſentiall, concerning their Rule &c. firſt of Obedience, Pouerty, Chaſtity, and of the eternall and ſtraite Incloſure. Secondly how they keep the diuine Office, as well by night as by day: then the manner of ſpeaking aſwel at the Grate as at the Speak-houſe. Thirdly of the gathering togeather of money, corne, oyle, and vvine. Fourthly of the ſeruice done to the ſicke, weake, and very aged. Fifthly of the number, richenes, and curioſity in habits and cloathings. Sixthly the obſeruances of abſtinence and faſtes: & of negligences of thoſe which rule. Seauenthly, of the Diſcreet Siſters, and of the Portreſſes. Eightly, of the Obedience and rebellion of the ſubiects.

Ninthly

Ninthly, of the obseruance of their Rule, and life, and of these present Ordinances. Tenthly, of the peace and vnity to be kept by the chaine of perpetuall Charity. Eleuenthly of the frequentation of the Sacrament of Pennance, and of the holy Sacrament of the Aultar. Twelthly, to enquire how the sacrifice of holy prayer and deuotion is cõtinued, and preserued in the Couent.

15. If any one or more should legitimately be found failing in any of these aforesaid thinges, or any thing which might be otherwise notoriously defectiue, that then she be duely corrected and punished according to discretion, zeale of charity, and loue of Iustice; and also according as the offence

hath bin committed more often.

¶ BY THE HELP OF these Declarations, Constitutions, and ordinances, we trust by the grace of God, to haue sufficiently prouided for your estate; the which by these present writings we doe send vnto you all, and vnto euery one of you, that you feruently & efficaciously fulfill, and accomplish them. And you ought by so much the more diligently to keepe and obserue them, by how much, we do assuredly iudge that by the true & entiere obseruation thereof, you shall gaine & enioy the fruit which is great, pretious, incomparable, and glorious.

And to the end, that the said Ordinances may be of greater authorithority, and receaued of you with greater deuotion and humility, we haue caused them to be signed, strengthened, and fortifyed, with the accustomed solemnities, as with reuiewing, examination, approbation, and the annexion of the Seale of our Office.

Giuen at *Geneua* in the Prouince of *Burgundy*, the yeare of our Lords Incarnation 1434. the eight and twentith day of September, and the third yeare of the Popedome of our holy Father Pope *Eugenius* the fourth, as also the third yeare of the holy Councell of *Basil*, gathered and assembled for the reformation of the Estates, and to procure peace betweene Princes, and for the extirpation of Heresies in which Councell these present Ordi-

Ordinaunces, and Declarations were viewed, examined, and approued.

Agayne renewed, and authorized by the Reuerend Father, F. Bingnus à Genua, *Generall of the whole Order of our Holy Father* S. Francis, *this present yeare of our Lord* 1622. *the* 22. *of Ianuary.*

An

An Exhortation for the better Obseruance of these present Constitutions, adioyned & approued by the Reuerend Father, F. Benignus à Genua *Minister-General of the holy Order of the Seraphicall Father S.* Francis.

DEERLY beloued in our Lord Iesus. It is not our intentiō to oblige you to your forsaid constitutiōs vnder paine of any sin, but only so much as God, your Rule, and the Church doth oblige

blige and bind you : Neuertheleſſe we wil and ordaine, that the tranſgreſſours of them be ſharply corrected ; and if the Abbeſſes ſhould be negligent to obſerue them , or to cauſe them to be obſerued, or to correct the tranſgreſſours, ſhe ſhall be ſeuerely reprehended , & inioyned Pennance according to the greatnes of her fault by the Prouincialls or Viſitours . For your holy Mother S. *Clare* being at the article of death , hath left the large benediction of the holy Trinity, togeather with her owne Motherly Benedictiõ vnto the true zealators and obſeruers of her Rule , and of the holy Pouerty. Wherefore you ought to endeauour diligently to imbrace and obſerue with affectionate & ſincere loue the perfection

which

which is expressed and taught you in the said Rule, and in these holy Ordinances, laying aside all negligence and tepidity. And because to serue God with no higher intention then to auoide paine, appertaineth only vnto base seruile spirits and hirelings, and to doe things pleasing to his diuine Maiesty purely for his honour and glory, and to giue good example vnto others, for such like respectes, belongeth to the true Children of God; we exhort you all in our Lord Iesus to take heed that you doe not make little account of the transgressing of these present Constitutions, in respect that they are not obligatory vnder paine of sin as we haue before said; but consi-sidering of what spirit & perfection they are, endeauour to obſerue them inuiolably, as the Lawes, Orders & Statutes of your Religion. Whereby you ſhall add more glory to your Crowne, by meanes of ſuch holy indeauours, and make your ſelues confomable to the Son of God, who not being obliged or bound to the Lawes which he had made, would neuertheleſſe obſerue them for the good of others. Seeke then to attaine vnto the ſoueraigne eſtate of your Religion, by inforcing your ſelues to put in execution thoſe things which are contayned in theſe preſent Conſtitutions; ſeing it appertayneth vnto good & loyall Seruants not to content thẽſelues with the fulfilling of thoſe thinges only, which their Maiſters comand them with treatnings, but also to seeke and desire to doe, and accomplish all such thinges which they thinke any waies to be pleasing and gratefull to their Maysters.

We doe therfore in the Charity of our Lord Iesus, exhort all the Sisters of this holy Order present and to come, that in all affaires & occasions they will keep before their eyes the holy Ghospell, the Rule which they haue promised to God, the holy and laudable customes, the memorable examples of Saints of their Order, in particular of their founders, drecting all their thoughts, words, and works, to the honor & glory of God and the health of their soules, & so doing, the holy Ghost will instruct them in all things.

Rayſe, therfore your eyes and thoughts vnto our Sweet Redeemer Ieſus, and hauing vnderſtood his holy wil and pleaſure, inforce your ſelues to pleaſe him not only in not contemning theſe preſent Conſtitutions (for the cōtempt of them were no ſmall ſin) but alſo auoiding and caſting aſide for his loue all negligence in their obſeruance. For they will help you not only to accompliſh intierly your holy Rule which you haue vowed, but alſo the diuine Law & Euangelicall couſailes, and obtaine you the grace of God by Ieſuschriſt which will deliuer you from many perills. In labours your conſolation will abound, and you ſhalbe able to doe all thinges in him, to wit, in Ieſus Chriſt, who is Almighty

mighty, and will comfort you, and giue you vnderstāding in al things, who is the wisdom of God, and giueth abondantly to euery one, and also vvill affoard you force and strength, seeing that it is he only who is the strength, and the vvord that beareth all.

Call often to mind (my deere Sisters in our Lord Iesus) that holy memorable Theme on which our Seraphicall Father, made a most worthy Sermon vnto a great multitude of Brothers, to wit, *Great things we haue promised to God, but greater God hath promised to vs: Let vs thē keep what we haue promised, & with inflamed desires, let vs aspyre to come vnto those goods which are promised vs: the pleasures of this world are short, but those infernall paynes which we get by following them, perpetuall. The sufferances we indure for the loue of Iesus Christ, and the Pennance we imbrace for him, will last a little while; but the glory which God will giue vs for them, shalbe without end: many are called to the Kingdome of God, but few are choosen, because few doe follow Iesus Christ in sincerity of hart: but in the end God wil giue to euery one the recōpence of his workes, as well to the good, as to the euill, eyther glory & happynes, or confusion and eternall fire.* Hitherto are the wordes of Saint Francis, the which deere Sisters may very fitly be applyed vnto you, for those thinges vvhich you haue promised: & although they be great, yet are they small in comparison of the eternall recompence which God will giue

you

you if you be faithfull obferuers of them. Goe forward then, and obferue them couragioufly, and doe not diftruft of your forces, feing the eternall Father, who hath created you, & called you to obferue the Euangelicall perfection, knowing well your naturall frailty, will not only make you ftrong and able, with his help, but alfo giue you his Fatherly gifts, in fo great multitude add abundance, that furmounting ouer all difficulties you fhal be able not only to obey his deerly beloued Sonne, but alfo to follow and imitate him with exceeding great ioy & fimplicity of hart; contemning perfectly thefe vifible temporall thinges, and alwaies afpiring vnto thofe which are heauenly, & eternall in Iefus Chrift, God and man, the true light and splendour of the glory of the eternal light, the mirrour without spot, the Image of God constituted by the eternall Father, Iudge, Law-giuer and Sauiour of men, vnto whome the Father and the holy Ghost doe giue witnes.

Wherefore, as in him are all our merits, our examples of life, our aide, fauours, and rewardes; so likevvise let all our thoughts, meditations, and imitations, be in him; & vnto them that so doe, all thinges will be sweet, pleasant, easy, light, holy & perfect. For he is the light and expectation of nations, the end of the Law, the saluation of God the Father of the world to come, and finally our hope made vnto vs, Wisdome,

Iustice,

Iustice, Sanctification, and Redemption: who liueth & raigneth with the Father & the Holy Ghost one coeternall, consubstantiall, and coequall God, to whom be euerlasting praise, honour, & glory. Giuen at Paris in our Couent of the *Aue Maria*, this 22. of Ianuary 1622.

Fr. Benignus à Genua
Vicar-Generall.

THE OBLIGATION OF THE RVLE

Of our holy Mother S. Clare *vnder payne of Mortall Sinne.*

POPE Eugenius the 4. declareth that in the said Rule there is no other precept obliging vnder Mortall sin, then the vowes of Obedience, Pouerty, Chastity, Inclosure Election & Deposition of the Abbesse.

The

The Perfections of the Rule consist in six Seraphicall Winges, to wit, in totall Obedience, *in Euangelicall* Pouerty, *in immaculate* Chastity, *in profound* Humility, *in Pacificall* Simplicity, *in Seraphicall* Charity.

OBEDIENCE is a Vertue which hath three degrees: the first is Obedience by profession, which is when one doth accomplish the commaundment of God, or the Prelate, touching the exteriour. The second is Obedēce by Conformity, which is when the commandment is performed not alone in the exterior, but also without murmuration, according to the intention and wil of him that commandeth. The third is Obedience by vnion, by which he that is truly Obedient, hath no other respect but the pleasure and will of God.

2. Euangelicall Pouerty is a vertue that hath three degrees: the first is Pouerty by Profession, that is, to haue no right nor propriety in any thing whatsoeuer: the second, to retaine only the simple vse of things necessary, & rest cōtented with the most vild: the third, not to haue any affection, euen in thinges necessary, but by way of constraint to take the bare vse of them.

3. Chastity is a vertue that hath three degrees: the first, Chastity of body, by which all the exteriour members are restrained from any impure or suspicious act: the second

cond, chastity of hart, by which the hart is preserued from any dishonest or vncleane thought: the third, Chastity of the spirit by which we not only refraine from any dishonest loue, but also from al excessiue delectation or spirituall consolation.

4. Humility is a vertue that hath three degrees: the first is, Humility of knowledge, by the which man doth acknowledge to be vile and abiect in himselfe: the second is Humility of exhibitiõ, by which the interiour humility is expressed in the exteriour, as by the attire, by vvordes, and by vvill, and abiect workes: the third is Humility of affection, through vvhich a soule doth not only humble herselfe in the sight of God, but also in the sight

sight of men, desiring to be esteemed poore & abiect.

5 Simplicity is a vertue which hath three degrees: the first is simplicity of thoughts, that is, not to enter into higher cogitation then the vnderstāding is capable of, neyther of honours and wordly dignities, but to esteeme himselfe the most vnworthy to serue God of all others: the second, is Simplicity in words, auoiding all affected curiosity in speach, speking plainly without superfluity, which stil comes of an ill roote, to wit vanity: the third is Simplicity of vvorks, imploying our selues in no other but such as are simple and profitable. And a generall rule of this Vertue is to haue a pure, right, and simple intention: but Simplicity vvithout Pru-

Prudence is not of value: for God loueth those that walke in Prudence.

6. Charity is a vertue of three degrees: the first is to loue God not only for his benefits, but also for that he is most worthy of it: the second, is to loue our neighbour, not only for the loue of our neighbour but simply for the loue of God: the third, to loue our selues in labouring for vertue, our happines, and glory; not for our owne respect but for the loue of God, and to be pleasing vnto him.

Prayse of the Rule.

THE holy Father S. Francis, encouraging his Religious to the obseruance of the Rule, said

said, It was the booke of life: the fruit of wisdom: the marrow of the Ghospell: the hope of health: the path of saluation, the ladder by which one ascendeth to heauen: the key of Paradise: and the pledge of Eternall Peace.

Three Priuiledges, which our holy Father S. Francis obtayned of Almighty God.

POPE Gregory the Ninth said to haue vnderstood of the holy Father S. Francis, that Almighty God had graunted him three Priuiledges: the first that the more the Religious of his order did increase, the more he would prouide for them: the second that none should euer vnhappily dye in the habit,

habit: the third that whosoeuer should persecute his Order should be grieuously punished by Almighty God.

Three other Priuiledges which he sayd to haue receaued by the Seraphim, when as he appeared vnto him, in the mountayne of Auerne.

THE first, that his order should last to the day of Iudgment: the second that whosoeuer would liue wickedly in the Order should not indure long: the third that whosoeuer did loue his Order although a great sinner, he should receaue and obtaine mercy of Almighty God.

Seauē other Priuiledges which by an Angel were reuealed vnto the holy F. S. Francis in the Couent of S. Vrbane, to all that obserued his Rule and dyed in the Order.

THE first, that if their intention be good, they shal euer be gouerned by the holy Ghost: the second, that in this their perigrination they shall still be particularly defended, & in all their temptations also, from mortall sinne: the third, that the fire of Purgatory shall not detaine them after their death from the immediate inioying of euerlasting glory: the fourth, that they shall receaue in themselues that promise

of our Sauiour made vnto his A-
postles, of sitting on the twelue
seates to iudge the tribes of Israell:
the fifth that such as loue the Order Almighty God will increase his
graces, and blessinges towardes
them in this world and the next:
the sixth, that those who are enemies to his order, & do persecute
it without repenting, either their
life shal be shortned, or if it be long
it shalbe replenished with misery,
and after their death be eternally
lost: the seauenth that there shall e-
uer be Religious of good and holy
life, louers of the honor of God, &
their Religion in this Order.

Certayne Indulgences graunted amongst many others, by the soueraygne Bishops of Rome, vnto all the Religious of the Order of S. Francis.

THE Religious both men and women shall gaine a plenary both *à pæna & culpa*, frō paine & fault, on the daies of their Cloathing, Profession, and article of death: also at the article of death the Fathers & Mothers of the said Brothers & Sisters may haue the same giuen thē, by any lawful Cōfessor.

2. All the Religious that shall receaue the most holy Sacrament vpon all Sundayes throughout the yeare, all the feastes of our Blessed Sauiour, & of our Blessed Lady, of

the

the Saints of the order, shall gaine a plenary Indulgence. And if it happen that any could not confesse & communicate these dayes, their hindrance being lawfull, they may gaine the same indulgence if after being freed of that impediment, they confesse and communicate for that intention, notwithstāding the day of the feast be past.

3. The Religious who shall recite the Corone of our Lord, that is 33. *Pater Nosters*, and *Aue Maria*, in honour of the 33. years he liued in the world, or the Corone or Rosary of the Glorious Virgin Mary, contayning 72. *Aues*, with 7. *Pater Nosters*, and one *Pater Noster* and *Aue* for the Soueraigne Bishop, do gaine plenary Indulgence. Likewise the same is graunted as

often as they say the seauen Psalms and Letanies, the Gradual Psalms, the office of the dead, or assist at the Letanies of euery second Sunday in the moneth.

4. As often as the Religious eyther by day or night, in what place soeuer they be, shall recite six *Pater Nosters* and *Aues*, and *Gloria Patri*, fiue for the necessities of the Church, and the sixt for the Popes Holines, shall gaine the indulgẽces of the Stations of Hierusalem, of Rome, of S. Iames, and of Portiuncula.

5. Item reciting the Psalme *Exaudiat te Dominus in die tribulationis &c.* three *Pater Nosters* and *Aues*, for the Popes intention, they shall gaine all the Indulgences graunted by the Soueraigne Bishops,

to

to the Cōfraternity of the Rosary, to the Churches of our Blessed Lady of Loreto, of Mont-serat, and of Saint Iames de Compostella.

6. Euery time they say the *Angelus Domini* at the accustomed time when it ringeth, a plenary indulgence: and the like euery time they communicate. As often as they heare the Masse of the Cōception of our Blessed Lady, praying for his Holines and the vniuersall Church, is graunted a Plenary indulgence. Saying the diuine office, or the office of our Blessed Lady, besides all other Indulgences, they gaine 100. yeares of pardon.

7. Saying once euery day one *Pater Noster* and *Aue Maria*, calling deuoutly three times vpon the Holy Name of Iesus, they gaine

3000. yeares of Pardon.

8. It is graunted vnto the Sisters that foure times a yeare they may haue a generall absolution in full remission of all their sinnes whatsoeuer, and be restored to the estate of innocency, as fully as they could receaue it from his Holines: & the like is graunted them on euery feast of our Blessed Sauiour, our Blessed Lady, on the feast of S. Peter and S. Paul, S. Fracis, S. Clare, S. Catharine Queene and Martyr, the feast of All Saints, and euery day of the holy weeke: yet notwithstanding these graces will profit nothing, vnto those who should vpon presumption to gaine them, sin more freely. They may apply all priuiledges and indulgences graunted to thẽselues, vnto the

the faithfull departed. Note that for the gayning of these or any indulgences is requisite the applying of the intention for the same.

An examen of Conscience for a Religious Person.

VVHAT are his euill inclinations and bad customes, whēce they proceed, & what warre & exercise he vseth against them.

2. What Passions most raigne in him, and by what meanes he hath hitherto indeauoured to mortify them.

3. What are his principall, most frequent, and most troublesome temptations, and how he hath hitherto behaued himself in them.

4. If he be indifferent in accepting any imployment of the holy Religion, willingly accepting whatsoeuer is appointed him.

5. Whether God be the only Intention of all his actions, or if he seeke proper commodity or praise in his workes.

6. Whether he doe not prefer exteriour matters, as good qualities and naturall gifts and graces, before the study of vertue and perfection.

7. If he desire, and be most contented his Superiours should haue knowledge of all his faultes.

8. If he be confident and open harted to his Superiours, & confer with them in any necessary occasion of things touching the good of his soule.

9. Whe-

9. Whether he be truly vnited by affectionvnto his Superiors, or if he haue any auersion, & from whence it proceedes.

10. Whether he be not too familiar with some, and if that familiarity be not hurtfull to himself and the other party, and if by that occasiõ he loose not time, & disedify others.

11. If he loue and imbrace the interiour and exteriour mortifications, and rather those matters that be hũble & abiect, then of esteeme and credit.

12. If he obserue al this Rules & Constitutions, of which he maketh lesse esteeme, & for what reason.

13. If he desire truly to be penitent for all his faultes, truly confessing them with strong purpose of amendment.

14. If he make a particular examen euery day vpon one imperfection, and with what preparation he receaueth the holy Sacramēt: and how he frequenteth the holy exercise of prayer.

15. If his wordes & discourses in Recreation or otherwise, as also with secular be of edification: how he obserueth silence, and spendeth his time.

Twelue great Euills which come by Veniall sinnes.

FIRST, they doe so darken and obscure the eyes of our vnderstanding, that they cannot see almighty God. 2. They kill the feruour of dilection and diuine Charity. 3. They hinder our prayers and

and petitions from being heard by God. 4. They defile and spotte the soule. 5. They contristate the holy Ghost, and reioice the enemy. 6. They depriue vs of the sweet and amiable familiarity of our Blessed Sauiour. 7. They are a great cause and meanes of our fall into more grieuous sinnes. 8. They cause a soule to fall into great slouth and tepidity in all goodnes. 9. They weakē exceedingly the forces of the soule, from resisting her bad inclinations. 10. They incline our affections and desires to temporall matters. 11. They prolong and augment the paines in purgatory. 12. They exceedingly hinder vs from seeing & enioying the presence of God.

Nyne wayes by which we participate of the sinnes of others.

BY Counsell. 2. By commandment. 3. By consent 4. By procuration or persuasion. 5. By flattery. 6. By holding our peace of his fault of whome we ought to haue care. 7. To dissemble or not to reprehend, and hinder if we be thereunto obliged. 8. In participating of the matter, whereof such a sinne doth proceed. 9. In defending the fault of another.

Twelue fruits of the B. Sacrament.

IT not only maketh possible but also most easy the forsaking and leauing of all earthly & fading thinges.

2. It

2. It causeth great profit & aduancement in heauenly thinges.

3. It rayseth the soule aboue all things created.

4. It inforceth the spirit vnto all good.

5. It illuminateth and giueth light to the vnderstanding, in the knowledge of God.

6. It causeth an inflamed feruerous possession of the pure loue of God alone.

7. It is the consummation of al vertue & perfection.

8. It giueth the soule possession of the treasury of all goods & riches.

9. It causeth a continuall interiour ioy.

10. It indeweth her with a happy security & assurance, in seeing him

him in whome she belieueth.

11. A perfect peace beginning in this life & continuing for eternity.

12. A perfect vniō with almighty God, wherby the soule is made participant of all diuine perfection.

Twelue Euangelicall Counsayles.

POVERTY, wherby a Religious person is estranged from all terrestriall things.

2. Obedience without which no vertue is perfect.

3. Chastity which beautifieth and addorneth all other vertues.

4. Charity towardes our enemies, wherby all spirituall infection of any sinne is expelled.

5. Mansuetude, which (as sayth

S.

S. Ambrose) is the medicine of the hart, wherby the soule is illuminated by God Almighty, to knowne his secrets.

6. Mercy, which extendeth it selfe to the help of euery one without limite, entreth sweetly into the hart with pitty, & cleanseth it frõ all sinne.

7. The simple word alwaies fructifying in God, in purity of intention, in charity &c.

8. Shunning occasion of sinne, conducting the soule with prudency, and security to the purchase of vertue.

9. Right intention, which maketh all workes to proceed of humility, to the edification of our neighbour.

10. Conformity of the worke vnto

vnto the word, wherby all speciall instrūction is seriously, & with all profit accepted.

21. Auoiding of vnprofitable solicitude, therby better to attend vnto spiritual illuminations, which are obscured by earthly cares.

22. Fraternall Correction, which is a light that illuminateth the vnderstāding, according to that of the Apostle, saying, That which is corrected is made apparent by the light that followeth.

The Malediction of S. Francis.

BY thee O Eternall, and Heauenly Father, and all the celestiall Court, and by me most Vnvvorthy, be accursed all those Brethren, vvho by their euill example doe ruine and destroy the thinges vvhich thou hast built, and ceasest not to build, by so many holy Brethren of this Order.

FINIS.